YOUR
ENDOWMENT

GAIN GREATER JOY AND SATISFACTION
IN YOUR TEMPLE SERVICE

YOUR ENDOWMENT

GAIN GREATER JOY AND SATISFACTION
IN YOUR TEMPLE SERVICE

MARK A. SHIELDS

CFI
Springville, Utah

ISBN 13: 978-1-59955-287-3

Published by CFI, an imprint of Cedar Fort, Inc., 2373 W. 700 S., Springville, UT 84663
Distributed by Cedar Fort, Inc., www.cedarfort.com

LIBRARY OF CONGRESS CATALOGING-IN-PUBLICATION DATA

Shields, Mark A. (Mark Alan)
  Your endowment / Mark A. Shields.
      p. cm.
  Includes bibliographical references.
  ISBN 978-1-59955-287-3 (acid-free paper)
  1. Temple endowments (Mormon Church) 2. Church of Jesus Christ of Latter-day Saints--
     Doctrines. I. Title.

BX8643.T4S53 2009
230'.9332--dc22

                                        2009029628

Cover design by Jen Boss
Cover photograph by Illya Plaksey
Cover design © 2009 by Lyle Mortimer
Edited and Typeset by Heidi Doxey

Printed in the United States of America

10 9 8 7 6 5 4 3 2

Printed on acid-free paper

ACKNOWLEDGMENTS

Thank you so deeply to Doug Clark
for the inspiration, motivation, encouragement, and doctrinal
consultation that made this project possible.

Special thanks also to my wife, Cami, and my father, Gordon,
for all of the help in editing and advising throughout the project
and for Cami's wonderful picture of our daughter, Heidi,
gazing at the Salt Lake temple.

Finally, thank you to Jennifer Hughes for the picture and her
help editing and to Ruth Hyde for her editing help as well.

CONTENTS

CHAPTER 1

INTRODUCTION

THE PARABLE OF THE PUZZLE

One day, a package arrived at a young woman's doorstep. Anxious to see what it was, the young woman opened the package and found it full of dozens of oddly shaped puzzle pieces. She was understandably curious, so she anxiously began assembling the pieces to learn what they meant. However, this puzzle quickly proved frustrating to the young woman because there was no picture to show how the assembled puzzle was supposed to look. Without the picture, she had no idea how to put the pieces together, so her interest soon declined. No one could blame her for wanting a guide of some sort to see what the pieces would look like when they were properly put together. Somewhat frustrated and confused, she put the pieces away.

Some time later, the young woman received another package at her doorstep. She anxiously opened this package and found a beautiful picture with no other explanation. Although it was beautiful, she had never seen anything like it before. She didn't know what to think. So, even though it was a beautiful picture, it meant little to her because it was so different and unfamiliar. As with the package she received earlier, she soon lost interest and put it away.

After awhile, she remembered the package of puzzle pieces she had received earlier. *Could there be a connection between the two packages?* she wondered.

She searched for the puzzle pieces she had put away earlier. When she found them, she tried to fit them together any way she could, now that she had an idea of how the final picture was supposed to look. It took her years to assemble the puzzle, and as she did she began to see and understand her picture better and better. After many years, she finally finished assembling the pieces. The shapes of the individual pieces disappeared and a beautiful painting emerged. It was no longer a puzzle, but a wonderful and original masterpiece. It was even more beautiful than the picture she had used to guide her in the assembly. She recognized what was in the puzzle picture. It was heaven.

The Package with the Puzzle

The temple endowment is comprised of many puzzle pieces, so to speak. Many of these pieces come to us in the endowment itself, but a great many pieces also come to us in the scriptures and the inspired words of church leaders. This is the first package received by the young woman, and it is actually more than one package. In fact, it's a series of packages arriving at our spiritual doorsteps throughout our lives. Until we are able to fit these pieces together and see the finished product, it will remain a puzzle to us.

The Package with the Picture

Think of going through the temple as the second package, which contained the picture. It is a beautiful experience, but many do not see the beauty in it because they find it unfamiliar, different, and perhaps even unrecognizable. Because of this lack of familiarity, they may view the temple experience as unfulfilling or as a mystery never to be understood.

Even though the picture is laid out in front of us in the temple, we do not comprehend the magnificence and grandeur of that picture. We don't realize the heavenly vision that is set before us. This can happen because we don't understand the meaning of the individual puzzle pieces and how they go together. It seems strange that we could have both the puzzle pieces and the final picture laid before us and still not recognize what we are looking at. The temple and the endowment will remain a mystery until we learn to better understand what the Lord is showing and teaching us.

The Role of This Book in the Parable

Think of this book as a guide to help you identify and assemble the pieces to create a clear picture. This book identifies many pieces of the puzzle, but certainly not all of them. It will help you find and recognize many more pieces in the scriptures, the inspired words of church leaders, and in the temple itself. It will also help you understand where the pieces go and how they fit together. It is a bridge that is meant to connect the two packages in the parable. I hope that when we have finished putting the pieces together, more of the finished product will be revealed, and you will recognize the temple as the gate to heaven. As you continue to receive and understand more pieces of the puzzle throughout your life, you will see more of the final picture, and it will only become more clear and beautiful to you.

The lessons of the temple are presented to us repeatedly before we finally understand them and they truly sink in. This is because the Lord teaches us by repetition. With that in mind, this book is meant to be repetition-friendly. It's short enough to be read and reread. It also has summary points at the end of each chapter for quick reference and easy repetition.

Regardless of how many times you read this, or any other book, to learn about the temple, the best guide to identifying the puzzle pieces and fitting them together will always be the Holy Ghost. No book can substitute for the worthiness, faith, and prayer that invite the Spirit and open our understanding of the temple.

Jesus Christ Is the Central Piece

The first lesson to be learned about the temple is that Jesus Christ is the most important piece of the puzzle. He fits right in the middle of the puzzle and extends through every other piece. "For through [Christ] we both have access by one Spirit unto the Father. Now therefore ye are no more strangers and foreigners, but fellowcitizens with the saints, and of the household of God; And are built upon the foundation of the apostles and prophets, Jesus Christ himself being the chief corner *stone;* In whom all the building fitly framed together groweth unto an holy temple in the Lord" (Ephesians 2:18–21; emphasis added).

As we identify and fit the pieces together, they will all point to the Savior and His Atonement. Simply put, coming to the temple is coming to Christ.

Putting the Pieces Together

If you have already gone through the temple, you have received the second package containing the final picture. You may not understand or recognize everything that is captured in that picture, but you are seeking that understanding. Because you have already received the picture and many of the puzzle pieces, this book will probably make more sense to you than to those who have not yet been through the temple. For those of you who have not yet received your endowment and the second package, do not worry. When you do receive it, you will have an understanding of the puzzle pieces that will help you recognize the beauty and the lessons of the endowment.

In the parable, it took years to put all of the pieces together. This is the way the Lord teaches (see 2 Nephi 28:30). Don't be frustrated by this sometimes slow process. In fact, as you put the pieces together, you will find that the Lord continues to send package after package of puzzle pieces throughout your life as you are ready for them. These additional packages are a blessing, not a frustration. The Lord designed the temple endowment in such a way that we would never stop learning from it. He wants us to keep going to the temple, not just so He can continue teaching us, but also so that we can serve the rest of His children who weren't fortunate enough to receive the endowment in mortality.

ON PREPARING TO ENTER THE TEMPLE

When we teach about the temple in the Church, the topics of discussion are usually the importance of the temple and temple work, the blessings of temple work, or sometimes the history of temples. While we are all taught that the temple is a holy and essential part of the plan of salvation, remarkably few of us are properly prepared to enter the temple and receive our endowment. We simply are not taught to think deeply and understand that the most meaningful lessons of the plan of salvation are taught in the temple. We are not taught to recognize the puzzle pieces, so to speak, so we don't see the finished product for what it is.

A story about David O. McKay, the ninth president of the Church, sums up this concern:

> When the Los Angeles Temple building program was commenced, President McKay called a meeting of the stake presidents of the temple district. During this meeting, President McKay took occasion to express his feelings about the holy endowment. He indicated how some years before, a niece of his had received her ordinances in the house of the Lord. He had learned that shortly before that experience she had been initiated into a sorority at the local university. She had the crassness to say that she found the sorority initiation superior in effect and meaning to her than the endowment.
>
> President McKay was open and frank with his audience about the experience of one in his own family with the endowment. He wasn't worried about their audible gasps. With characteristic aplomb, he paused and then said, "Brothers and sisters, she was disappointed in the temple. Brothers and sisters, I was disappointed in the temple. And so were you." Then he said something incredibly important that

should be engraven on all our souls. "There are few, even temple workers, who comprehend the full meaning and power of the temple endowment. Seen for what it is, it is the step-by-step ascent into the Eternal Presence." Then he added, "If our young people could but glimpse it, it would be the most powerful spiritual motivation of their lives!"[1]

If a prophet of God is not ashamed to admit that his family was not properly prepared to enter the temple, none of us should be either.

In this respect, I have something in common with President McKay, and the hundreds of young men and women he mentioned. Despite appearances, I was not well prepared to enter the temple. I was born and raised in a wonderful family in the Church. I faithfully attended all my meetings growing up. I graduated from seminary. I took advantage of every opportunity as a youth to go to the temple and do baptisms for the dead. I even went along with my parents sometimes when they went to the temple. I would wait outside, walking around the grounds and taking in the spirit I felt there. I learned to love the temple from a very young age, years before I was able to enter it.

Still, I am the first to admit that I was under-prepared for the temple when I received my endowment. I was worthy to be there, but I had remarkably little understanding of what I was experiencing. I never questioned the experience, as the Lord had well proven to me through the years that this was in fact His church. I knew the temple was the Lord's way of teaching me, but I didn't understand what or how He was trying to teach me. The puzzle pieces made little sense to me, and the endowment was an unfamiliar painting.

What I *did* understand was the feeling I had while receiving my endowment. I had never felt so *clean* in my life. But, again, I didn't understand the experience, so I obviously didn't benefit from it nearly as much as I could have or should have.

BECOMING BETTER PREPARED TO ENTER THE TEMPLE

We should not be content with our lack of understanding of the temple. It is the most sacred place on Earth. It is where we receive the highest ordinances and make the highest covenants in mortality. The Lord does not want us to go through mortality without understanding the temple!

President Kimball once said, "If you understood the ordinances of the House of the Lord, you would crawl on your hands and feet for thousands of miles in order to receive them!"[2]

The blessings of the temple are so great that it could take us a lifetime just to understand them. If we could accelerate that understanding process a little, perhaps we could instead spend a lifetime cherishing, living with, and sharing those blessings.

This invitation to prepare and understand better is open to those entering the temple for the first time as well as those who have spent years in the temple. As President McKay pointed out, even many temple workers do not truly understand the endowment.

UNDERSTANDING THE TEMPLE ACCORDING TO INSPIRED WORDS OF CHURCH LEADERS

This book will attempt to help you identify and arrange many pieces of the puzzle principally by referencing two quintessential quotes about the temple endowment that appear in virtually every Latter-day Saint writing on the subject. One is from Brigham Young, and the other is from James E. Talmage. These quotes are marvelous explanations of the purpose and sanctity of the temple experience. They give us many, many puzzle pieces.

Brigham Young on the Endowment:

"Let me give you a definition in brief. Your endowment is, to receive all those ordinances in the House of the Lord, which are necessary for you, after you have departed this life, to enable you to walk back to the presence of the Father, passing the angels who stand as sentinels, being enabled to give them the key words, the signs, and tokens, pertaining to the Holy Priesthood, and gain your eternal exaltation in spite of earth and hell."[3]

This is an outstanding summary of the endowment. However, the typical person entering the temple has been taught little to nothing about some of the concepts in President Young's definition prior to entering the temple. In fact, the very word "endowment" is something that few church members can truly define. These simply are not the subjects of a typical Sunday School lesson. Likewise, the concept of symbolism that the Lord uses to teach His greatest truths in the temple is not stressed or explained well in most church services either. These puzzle pieces are foreign to most of us, just like the picture we see in the temple.

James E. Talmage on the Endowment:

Elder Talmage's explanation of the endowment is more specific and yet also more broad than President Young's. It gives a synopsis of the endowment, summarizes covenants made in the endowment, and reiterates the sanctity and purpose of the endowment.

> The Temple Endowment, as administered in modern temples, comprises instruction relating to the significance and sequence of past dispensations, and the importance of the present as the greatest and grandest era in human history. This course of instruction includes a recital of the most prominent events of the creative period, the condition of our first parents in the Garden of Eden, their disobedience and consequent expulsion from that blissful abode, their condition in the lone and dreary world when doomed to live by labor and sweat, the plan of redemption by which the great transgression may be atoned, the period of the great apostasy, the restoration of the gospel with all its ancient powers and privileges, the absolute and indispensable condition of personal purity and devotion to the right in present life, and a strict compliance with gospel requirements. . . .
>
> The ordinances of the endowment embody certain obligations on the part of the individual, such as covenant and promise to observe the law of strict virtue and chastity; to be charitable, benevolent, tolerant, and pure; to devote both talent and material means to the spread of truth and the uplifting of the race; to

maintain devotion to the cause of truth; and to seek in every way to contribute to the great preparation that the earth may be made ready to receive her King,—the Lord Jesus Christ. With the taking of each covenant and the assuming of each obligation a promised blessing is pronounced, contingent upon the faithful observance of the conditions.

No jot, iota, or tittle of the temple rites is otherwise than uplifting and sanctifying. In every detail the endowment ceremony contributes to covenants of morality of life, consecration of person to high ideals, devotion to truth, patriotism to nation, and allegiance to God. The blessings of the House of the Lord are restricted to no privileged class; every member of the Church may have admission to the temple with the right to participate in the ordinances thereof, if he comes duly accredited as of worthy life and conduct.[4]

This description of the endowment mentions concepts and puzzle pieces that are more familiar to most members of the Church. It points specifically to the story of Adam and Eve. While Latter-day Saints are much more familiar with Adam and Eve than they are with some of the words in President Young's definition, many still need a deeper understanding of Adam and Eve in order to understand the temple. Adam and Eve and the Fall are extremely important puzzle pieces. If we put them in their right places, the rest of the picture takes shape much more easily.

Elder Talmage's definition also stresses the ordinances and covenants of the temple and the blessings that flow from them. These puzzle pieces are fairly well discussed in the Church, but, again, we have a lot to learn about how they fit together to complete the puzzle.

Keep in mind what we have been well taught about the temple: It is the most sacred place on Earth. The temple experience, in its fullest, is the most sacred experience available to the Father's children on Earth. Words are often not enough to describe any joyous experience in life, much less the experience of visiting the most sacred place on Earth. It would be extremely difficult to find words that can do justice to the most sacred experience available to us. These explanations from President Young and

Elder Talmage are the best words we have on the subject of the temple, but they cannot explain everything. They are necessarily condensed. To the sincere seeker of truth, they should raise at least as many questions as they answer.

Still, both President Young's and Elder Talmage's summaries may be condensed even further by saying that the endowment allows us to put the Atonement into full effect in our lives. The Atonement is truly the largest and most important piece of the puzzle, and it is right at the heart of the final masterpiece.

To identify and assemble the pieces of the puzzle, we will discuss the temple as a model of the plan of salvation. We will address the greatest preparation for entering the temple, which is to become worthy. We will also address the blessings, covenants, and ordinances of the temple. Not coincidentally, these are the same subjects discussed in the Church's temple preparation class. However, in this book we have the luxury of going into greater detail about these puzzle pieces, particularly Adam and Eve and the role they play in the temple's teachings about the plan of salvation. We also have the luxury of examining the meaning of some of the words associated with the temple experience.

SUMMARY

- Far too many people in the Church don't understand the temple endowment, whether they are going through for the first time or have been attending for years. There is no shame in admitting this, but there is more we can do to prepare ourselves to understand the temple experience.
- This book is written specifically to help everyone—the first time temple attendee and the temple worker alike—understand the endowment better.
- This is a guide to help identify, recognize, and fit together the pieces of the puzzle, so that we will recognize the final picture and see it as heaven. This book will identify many,

but certainly not all, of the puzzle pieces and help you understand where and how the pieces fit together.

- President Brigham Young described the endowment as receiving the tools we need to return back to our Heavenly Father after we have left Earth.

- Elder James E. Talmage described the endowment as a panorama of the plan of salvation, starting with the Creation and the Fall and leading through to our redemption. He also spoke of the covenants and ordinances that comprise the endowment and that prepare us to meet the Lord.

- Both of these descriptions of the endowment may be summarized by saying that the temple exists for us to fully apply the Atonement in our lives.

INVITATION

Enjoy.

Notes

1. Andrew Ehat, "'Who Shall Ascend into the House of the Lord?' Sesquicentennial Reflections of a Sacred Day: 4 May 1842," *Temples of the Ancient World*, 58.
2. Ibid., 59.
3. Brigham Young, *Discourses of Brigham Young*, 416.
4. James E. Talmage, *The House of the Lord*, 83–84.

CHAPTER 2

UNDERSTANDING THE WORDS THAT ARE CENTRAL TO THE TEMPLE ENDOWMENT

Many important words that are associated with the temple experience are translated from Hebrew in the Old Testament and Greek in the New Testament. You will recognize several of these words from the quotes by President Young and Elder Talmage in the last chapter. These quotes are the best starting point we have for understanding the temple experience, so understanding the full meaning of the words in these quotes is critical. Many of the words are themselves pieces of the puzzle that we're trying to assemble.

Some of these words lose much of their true meaning when they are translated to English. They are better understood when we study what they mean in their original form. Some of these words are actually names that have a deeper meaning associated with them.

Those who have already received their endowment will recognize these words. But many people have perhaps spent years or decades of temple worship without really understanding or appreciating the true meaning of these words. Hopefully, these definitions will set off a light bulb, and you will see your familiar temple experience in a new light.

Those who are preparing to go through the temple will benefit greatly from having an understanding of these words beforehand. Look for these words as they unfold before you in the temple, in the scriptures, and in other divinely inspired messages. If you understand these words ahead of time, then the light bulb can go on for you the first time you go through the temple.

Simply understanding the true message of some of these words will help you comprehend and treasure your temple experience so much more than you would without this understanding.

A word of caution—notice how these specific words are used by Elder Talmage and President Young in their quotes, which have been published openly in the Church for many decades. From their use, we may infer that it is all right to discuss them in a general sense, as Elder Talmage and President Young have done. However, notice, particularly with President Young, that he does not give specific examples of, say, a token or a sign in the context of the temple. In other words, President Young tells us that signs, tokens, and so forth are necessary for us to return to our Father in Heaven, but he is careful not to say more than that. These are general definitions, and we must be careful to limit our discussion to the same generalities expressed by President Young and Elder Talmage. We do not, should not, and, if we value sacred things, *must* not discuss the specific applications of these concepts outside of the temple.[1]

Going back to our parable of the puzzle, we do not discuss the specifics of the second package—the picture that showed how the pieces should look when they are assembled. That picture is only received in the temple itself. Likewise, many of the pieces of the puzzle are only found in the temple itself.

The following words are grouped in order of subject and not alphabetically.[2]

Adam—In Hebrew, Adam means "mankind."[3] In this sense, *Adam* is a generic term used for humanity. It is not gender specific, so it refers to both men and women.

In reality, Adam is the prototype human. The scriptures begin with the Creation and the story of Adam. The temple is no different and follows the same pattern, as noted by Elder Talmage. It is no coincidence that the Lord begins his teachings in holy writ and in the temple drama with the same account of the Creation and Adam and Eve.

The roles played by Adam and Eve are some of the most important pieces of the puzzle that we can identify and fit together. As Alonzo Gaskill summarizes:

> Why all of the Adamic parallels? Because Adam and Eve are our pattern. Their story is ours. Noah, Abraham, covenant Israel, and you and I are to consider ourselves as if we were Adam and Eve. We are to see the story of the Fall as the story of our fall. Thus, so much of our lives—and so much of the lives of the ancient patriarchs and prophets—seems saturated in symbols of the paradise that was willingly given up in the hopes of obtaining an inheritance in the celestial kingdom.
>
> The fact of the matter is that the story of the Fall—as told in scripture and the temple—is intended to give us more detail regarding our personal falls (as weak and sinful mortals) than about the Fall of historical figures, Adam and Eve. Each of the inspired, authorized accounts have been couched in such a way as to serve as a message about *our* need for obedience, the consequences of *our* sins, and *our* desperate need for a Savior to redeem us from *our* fallen condition. To misunderstand this is to misunderstand the Fall.[4]

I have often wondered why of all the subjects of the restored gospel the Fall of Adam is the subject of the second Article of Faith. I could understand readily if it were the eleventh or twelfth, but why the second? I believe the answer is, in part, that we have to understand the Fall if we are to understand the plan of salvation. If we view Adam as anything less than our first earthly father and our role model in fulfilling the plan of salvation, we will never understand our place in eternity and the purpose of mortality. We will not understand the path that we must travel through all the trials of mortality back to the tree of life. We will certainly not learn the lessons of the temple.

Adding the feminine ending *ah* to the root word Adam yields the word *adamah*, which means "earth." It is clear that there is a close relationship between Adam (mankind) and Earth. Man's time on Earth is the key and pivot point to his returning to the presence of God and again being like God.

Michael—Michael is the sum of three separate Hebrew words—*Mi* means "who," *cha* means "like," and *El* means "God." Michael therefore means, "who is like God."[5]

Elder Bruce R. McConkie taught that Michael was the pre-mortal name of Adam.

> In the eternal worlds, the firstborn spirit offspring of the Father was Jehovah, who is Christ (Abraham 2:7–8; JST Exodus 6:3; Psalms 83:18; Isaiah 12:2; 26:4, 19; D&C 110:1–10; Moroni 10:34). He was preeminent (Abraham 3:24, 27). Standing next to Christ was the great spirit, Michael (*Teachings of the Prophet Joseph Smith*, p. 157). Michael was prepared and chosen and sent here as Father Adam, the first man of all men, the first flesh upon the earth (Moses 3:7), the head of the human race, and the presiding high priest, under Christ, over all the earth.[6]

Significantly, Michael is also the *post-mortal* name of Adam (D&C 78:16).

As I see it, there is an unmistakable lesson in these names: Michael (who is like God) came to Earth where he was given the name of Adam (mankind). After fulfilling his earthly ministry by making and keeping covenants, he is called by another name, which is actually a restoration of his former name, Michael. This name teaches that he is again like God. The temple takes us on this journey, through the experience of Adam and Eve, from the pre-mortal existence, through mortality, to being like God.

As he progressed through the eternities, his name was changed to reflect his nature and his station in the Lord's plan. He progressed from being like God in the pre-mortal world, to being mortal, to again being like God as he fulfilled the purpose of his earthly mission. Remember, Adam is not just another person; he is our role model. Our goal is to follow the same pattern so that we can return to our Father in Heaven and be like Him. This is done through a progression of ordinances and covenants—divine promises made and divine promises kept. The change of names represents mankind's pre-mortal origin and post-mortal destiny that is made possible through the Atonement.

If we were to map this concept, it would look like this:

MICHAEL: Who is like God
ADAM: Mankind on Earth
MICHAEL: Who is like God

The concept of becoming like God is not a uniquely LDS doctrine. Contrary to what the Church's critics say, there is nothing new or unholy about the concept of man becoming like God. The doctrine did not originate with Joseph Smith, Brigham Young, or Lorenzo Snow. The doctrine is actually found quite clearly in the Sermon on the Mount where the Lord commanded us to be perfect, even as our "Father which is in heaven is perfect" (Matthew 5:48). This commandment is a clear charge to become like God, and we can rest assured that the Lord would not give us a commandment that is impossible.

The point at which Adam changes direction from the Fall and begins to become again like God is described by King Benjamin. "For the natural man is an enemy to God, and has been from the fall of Adam, and will be, forever and ever, unless he yields to the enticings of the Holy Spirit, and putteth off the natural man and becometh a saint through the atonement of Christ the Lord, and becometh as a child, submissive, meek, humble, patient, full of love, willing to submit to all things which the Lord seeth fit to inflict upon him, even as a child doth submit to his father" (Mosiah 3:19).

The Atonement is the center focal point of this journey from the Fall back to the Father. Man continues to be an enemy to God and to grow further from being like God until he comes to Christ and begins to apply the Atonement. Using our vocabulary terms, when Adam meets the Son of God, he begins his journey back to being Michael. Adding this principle into the diagram, it begins to look like this:

> *MICHAEL:* Who is like God
> *ADAM:* Mankind after the Fall
> → *CHRIST:* The Atonement reverses the Fall
> *MICHAEL:* Mankind having applied the Atonement
> and becoming again like God

The Atonement is the center of the plan of salvation and man's journey from God, to mortality, and then back to God. By no coincidence, it is also the focal point of the temple. If we do not understand that Christ is the center of the Plan and the center of the temple experience, we will miss the point. This progression of Michael to Adam through Christ back to Michael is the essence of the Plan. It represents man's origin as a son of God, man's present state in mortality, man's potential to be like God, and the Savior who makes it all possible.

Eve—The name Eve comes from the Hebrew word *chavvah*, which means "living."[7] *Chavvah* is a feminine adjective. In that sense, Eve represents feminine life and is the mother of all human life on Earth.

Cherubim—This curious word is closely associated with Adam and Eve, as "cherubim" were placed to guard the way of the tree of life after Adam and Eve had eaten from the tree of knowledge of good and evil (Genesis 3:24). This is a Hebrew word that really doesn't translate perfectly into English as far as we can tell. That is why it arrives in its Hebrew form throughout the Bible, the Book of Mormon, and the Pearl of Great Price.

According to Joseph Fielding McConkie, cherubim are "sentinels."[8] This word is familiar from Brigham Young's quote on the endowment. Sentinels or cherubim are the ones we must pass to return to the Father's presence. To apply President Young's quote regarding "sentinels," consider that cherubim were woven into the veil of the ancient temple that guarded the Holy of Holies (Exodus 26:31). The Holy of Holies represents the presence of God. Therefore, cherubim guard the veil to the symbolic presence of God.

Cherubim not only guard the opening to the Holy of Holies, but they are also found inside the Holy of Holies, guarding the Ark of the Covenant on its cover (Exodus 24:18–21). The mercy seat was the top or covering of the Ark of the Covenant in ancient temple worship (Exodus 24:17). According to the footnote in the LDS edition of that same part of the King James Bible, "mercy seat" may be translated as "atonement cover." The "atonement cover" was found in the Holy of Holies and represented the throne and direct presence of God. "And there I will meet with thee, and I will commune with thee from above the mercy seat, from between the two cherubims which are upon the ark of the testimony, of all things which I will give thee in commandment unto the children of Israel" (Exodus 25:22). This emphasizes the connection between the Atonement, achieving holiness, and returning to the presence of God. It is the holiest place within the temple itself and the point of direct communion with God. Therefore, cherubim guard the presence of God in every respect, including our access to the Atonement, as represented by the "atonement cover" or mercy seat.

Endowment—Comes from a Latin word that means the conferral or bestowal of a gift.[9] The "heavenly gift" spoken of in the scriptures may be a reference to this definition (4 Nephi 1:3; Ether 12:8). Our endowment is the gift from God that enables us to return to His presence.

In Greek, the word carries a most interesting definition. In Luke 24:49, the Lord spoke of his disciples being "endued with power from on high." *Endue* is the Greek form and root of the word that we have as "endow." It means "to clothe."[10] In his journals, Joseph Smith used the words "endument" and "endowment" interchangeably, so it appears that the Savior was referring to the same concept in Luke 24 that we now have in our modern temples through Joseph Smith.[11]

This is a great word to ponder. Of all the words the Lord could have chosen to represent and describe the temple experience, we have a word that means "to clothe." The lesson from this word choice is that the act of being clothed is a central theme of the temple experience.

What does clothing do for us?

It warms us. It protects us. It is literally what we keep closest to ourselves. It distinguishes us. It even has the capacity to uplift us. For example, we wouldn't picture a king or a queen dressed in jeans, shorts, or even Sunday dress clothes. A king and queen, when acting in their position of royalty, would be expected to wear magnificent and majestic robes with regal embellishments. So, don't expect anything casual or even Sunday-best about the endowment of the temple. The temple endowment does not bestow a typical or worldly level of distinguishing, blessing, or protection; it brings an eternal level.

An act of clothing was also the first act performed by the Lord after Adam and Eve partook of the fruit of the tree of knowledge of good and evil. "Unto Adam also and to his wife did the Lord God make coats of skins, and clothed them" (Genesis 3:21). According to the Genesis and Moses accounts, the Lord clothed Adam and Eve even before casting them out of the Garden of Eden (Genesis 3:21; Moses 4:27). This act qualifies as an endowment according to the true definitions of the word: It was a gift from the Lord (according to the Latin word leading to our English definition), and that gift was an article and act of clothing (according to the Greek definition). These scriptures therefore teach that the Lord actually gave Adam and Eve a kind of endowment to help them on their way to return to Him before they were even cast out from His presence.

It is also significant to note that this clothing was made of animal skins (Genesis 3:21; Moses 4:27). Animals must necessarily be killed before they are skinned. Since death did not exist before the Fall (Alma 12:24), these animals whose skins were given to Adam and Eve were likely the first creatures to die and, therefore, likely the first sacrifice offered. Genesis and Moses both state that it was "the Lord" who made the coats of skins for Adam and Eve. This suggests that it was likely the Lord Himself who performed the sacrifice.

Now, if the thought of Deity slaughtering and sacrificing an innocent animal such as a young lamb seems difficult to picture or accept, consider how Abraham must have felt when he had his beloved son Isaac on the altar with his arm raised to sacrifice him. Now consider how the Father must have felt while He permitted His Only Begotten to suffer in Gethsemane and to die on Golgotha. Who was better qualified to offer the first sacrifice on Earth? Who was better qualified to teach Adam and Eve the law of sacrifice and the symbolism in that law?

The coats of skins also served Adam and Eve as a constant reminder of the first sacrifice performed in the Garden of Eden.

The coats of skins, which most likely came from the sacrifice and death of an animal, would have also been a constant reminder—perhaps the ultimate reminder—of their own mortality that came with the Fall. Adam and Eve would have learned very quickly that they were completely dependent on the Atonement to deliver them from physical death. They wore the coats as a constant reminder of the Atonement and the permanent physical death that would await them if not for the Atonement.

The garment that is given as part of today's temple experience serves the same purpose of reminding us today. "Endowed members of the Church wear the garment as a reminder of the sacred covenants they have made with the Lord and also as a protection against temptation and evil. *How it is worn is an outward expression of an inward commitment to follow the Savior.*"[12] When Paul stated that he bore the marks of Christ in his body, he might have been referring to the same garments (Galatians 6:17).

This first sacrifice emphasizes the connection between the act of divine clothing (the endowment) and the principle of sacrifice. What was likely the first sacrifice on Earth led directly to the first endowment on Earth. Today, receiving the endowment leads us to the great and last sacrifice—the Atonement of Jesus Christ (Alma 34:10).

It is not an oversimplification to say that the temple exists so that we may fully put the Atonement into practice in our lives. Again, coming to the temple is coming to Christ.

Sacrifice—Sacrifice is associated with giving up one thing in exchange for something better. This notion is a lesson well served, but there is actually more to the meaning of the word. The word actually means "to make holy" or sacred. It comes from two Latin words, *sacer*, which means "holy" or "sacred," and *ficium*, which is based on the root *facere*, meaning "to make."[13] Portuguese and Spanish speakers will note that *sacer* forms the base for their words for "priest" and "priesthood." This is no coincidence. The great and last sacrifice by the Great High Priest is the only way we are made holy. Again, the ordinances and covenants of the temple are what gives us full access to the Atonement.

Atonement—The word "atonement" does not come to us from Latin, Greek, or Hebrew, but from old English. Because it comes from our native language, we don't have to translate it to understand it; we only need to break it down into its root words: At-one-ment, or in other words, to make as one or to make whole.[14]

The story of the Creation, as related in the book of Abraham, is a series of "divisions." The light was first divided from the darkness (Abraham 4:4, 14). Then the waters and expanse were divided (Abraham 4:6–7).

Man and woman were also divided, in a sense, as Eve was symbolically taken from Adam's rib (Abraham 5:17; Moses 3:21; Genesis 2:21).

With the Fall, the division continued. Physical death—a separation of the body and spirit—was introduced (Alma 12:23). Finally, a division between man and God resulted from the Fall. This is spiritual death (Alma 12:16, 32).

The Atonement exists to overcome all of these divisions or separations.

The word *atonement* only appears one time in the New Testament. The Greek word used there (*katallage*) comes from a root that means "to exchange."[15] Although Isaiah did not write in Greek, this Greek meaning applies beautifully to his description of the mission of the Lord as an "exchange" of "beauty for ashes, the oil of joy for mourning, the garment of praise for the spirit of heaviness" (Isaiah 61:3). In this sense, the Atonement is a type of exchange—of sin and repentance for holiness and forgiveness.

Other meanings for this Greek word are "restoration to the divine" or "reconciliation."[16] These too are poignantly illustrative examples of the Atonement, bringing mankind back to God and godliness by reconciling him with Deity.

The word "atonement" in one form or another appears in Hebrew more than eighty times in the Old Testament, either as *kippur* (a noun) or its root word *kaphar* (a verb). *Kaphar* is a remarkably transcendent word that means to expiate, condone, cancel, appease, cleanse, disannul, forgive, be merciful, pacify, pardon, to purge, to put off, or to reconcile.[17] When it comes to our sins, these are all words we hope to hear from the Lord at the day of judgment.

Of this group, the word "disannul" is particularly interesting. It is a double negative. It undoes an undoing, so to speak. This is a very illustrative way of describing the Atonement as the antidote to the Fall. Man began in the presence of God, and the Atonement serves to restore him to his former place or undoing his undoing, for lack of a better term.

Temple—The Hebrew form of "temple" is *heykal*, which means "palace."[18] A palace is a home for royalty. Those who go to the temple are given the opportunity to become royalty and make for themselves a home in the temple.

The English word for "temple" comes to us from a Latin and Greek root *tem* (as in "template") that denotes an intersection of a horizontal and vertical line.[19] The horizontal may be thought of as us, mankind here on Earth. The vertical may be thought of as representing God. In the temple, the horizontal (Adam, mankind) is brought into harmony with the vertical (God). The temple is literally where heaven meets Earth, where our will is brought into harmony and conformity with God's will. This is the same concept expressed in a cross, when we raise our arm to sustain someone or when a priesthood holder raises his arm in performing the ordinance of baptism: The horizontal and the vertical—mankind and God—are brought into harmony.

This root (*tem*) also symbolizes a "cutting" or "dividing"[20] between an inner and outer region. In this sense, the temple marks a division. However, this division is not between man and God, but between those who enter into covenant and those who do not enter into covenant. It is a selection process, and a divine one at that.

Profane—To be clear, we don't speak profanities in the temple, and you will likely never hear the word "profane" in the temple. This word is associated with foul language, which obviously has no place or part of the temple experience. However, there is a lesson in this word that helps put the temple into focus.

The word "profane" actually means "before" or "outside of the temple" in Latin (*pro* [before] + *fanum* [temple]).[21] The word actually pertains far more to sacred boundaries than it does to the language we use. When we speak of the temple or enter the temple, we are under a sacred obligation to do so with the greatest of respect and sanctity. Failing to treat the temple with its due reverence is a very real form of profanity. We should not allow something sacred to be dragged out of its proper and revered place. To do so is to cast pearls before swine.

This concept is remarkably well illustrated by the law of chastity. Marital relations, when within the bounds or the "temple" of marriage as set by the Lord, are a beautiful, wholesome, and essential part of the Lord's plan. However, when they are taken outside of the sacred bounds set by the Lord and the "temple" of marriage, they are among the most serious of sins.

The point here is to be careful to maintain sanctity. There are certain parts of the temple experience that are not to be discussed outside of the temple. At all times, reverence should be our guide in attending and discussing the temple.

There is great wisdom in the guidelines my father taught me about what should or should not be discussed outside the temple. If we read it in the scriptures or the writings of the brethren, we may safely, but reverently discuss it outside the temple. If the temple is the only place we hear of something, then it should be the only place we speak of it.

The definition of this word is also a lesson to exercise caution in choosing sources to learn of sacred subjects like the temple. For some reason, critics of the Church cannot seem to leave it alone. Many of those critics have spewed forth profanity by publishing holy subjects for all of the unprepared and unrespecting to see. Don't go after the profanity spread by the dregs of the world who have made a farce of their covenants. There are more than enough proper resources available to teach you about the temple.

Token—You should recognize this word from President Young's summary of the endowment. The definition of *token* is "to throw together" (derived from the Greek *sumbolon*, which is also the root word for *symbol*).[22] This definition may seem confusing by itself, as it makes little sense without its application.

The application of the word is an entirely different and very important lesson. "Contracting parties would break a *sumbolon*, a bone or a tally stick, into two pieces, then fit them together again later. Each piece would represent its owner; the halves 'thrown together' represent two separated identities merging into one."[23] The same thing was also accomplished with a raised seal made by making an impression in wax with a ring or stamp. Tokens were a physical proof of having entered into an agreement. Each party's part of the token would fit the other one's part of the token. The two halves of the token were "thrown together" as a personal emblem or proof of their agreement held by each party.

Simply put, a token is your physical proof of a contract. It is "something given as the symbol and evidence of a right or privilege, upon presentation of which the right or privilege may be exercised."[24] Each party to the agreement holds a unique half that is "thrown together" with the other party's unique half, and together they form a token.

A token was physically something small and otherwise unimpressive, but it represented so much more: a person's word and honor, a solemn agreement to do certain things, or even the right to a land of inheritance that would be passed down for generations from parent to child.

Using a stick to memorialize an agreement nowadays would be a foreign concept to us because we've replaced such tokens largely with written contracts. Because of our society, we don't attach the same meaning to a token that people in ancient days would have attached. Still, if we put ourselves in the shoes of the ancients, there is a great lesson to be learned by the concept of tokens, and we will be very slow to reject the concept as something foreign or insignificant.

Sign—This is another word you remember from President Young's endowment description. In Hebrew, the word for "sign" is exactly the same as the word for "token."[25] The two concepts are closely related, so the lessons about tokens also apply to signs. In the Old Testament, the same word was sometimes translated as "token" and other times translated as "sign." The word *owth* is also correctly translated as mark, flag, beacon, monument, omen, prodigy, evidence, and miracle.

There is an interesting message in this Hebrew word. It begins with an *aleph*, the first letter in the Hebrew alphabet, and ends with a *tav*, the last letter of the Hebrew alphabet. This may suggest a representation of the Lord Jesus Christ, who is called the Alpha and Omega, after the first and last letters of the Greek alphabet (Revelation 1:8, 11; 22:13). He is also called the First and the Last (Isaiah 41:4; 44:6; 48:12).

Therefore, in general terms, a sign may be correctly interpreted as a representation or identification of the Lord, especially of His Atonement. We come to know the Savior by keeping the commandments and putting the Atonement into practice in our lives (John 7:17; 17:3). Generally speaking, the signs of the Lord represent the process of putting the Atonement into practice and coming to know the Lord.[26]

OTHER IMPORTANT GOSPEL WORDS

Have you ever noticed how many important words in the gospel begin with the prefix "re"? We go to the temple to *re*ceive covenants, ordinances, and instructions. There we learn about the plan of *re*demption. Before we can enter the temple, we must *re*pent and obtain a *re*commend. When we take the sacrament, we promise to *re*member the Lord so that we can have His spirit with us. The list goes on and on, and it is hardly a coincidence that so many significant gospel words begin with this prefix.

The prefix *re* means "again" or "anew" in Latin. It suggests a return to a previous status or a repeating of an event. In many of these words, the prefix indicates that we are doing or getting something, even though we may have no recollection of doing or getting that thing the first time. For example, if we receive ordinances or covenants in the temple, when did we get them before? There is a distinct message in these words that draws us back to our pre-mortal existence and our heritage as children of God. Nowhere is that principle taught better than in the temple. There is something about these words that points us in the direction of Michael, even while we currently find ourselves in the position of Adam.

Receive—This is a Latin and old French word meaning to "take or get back."[27] We may correctly say that we receive gifts, ordinances, covenants, and the like in this world. However, following the true meaning of the word, we are really saying that we take or get these gifts, ordinances, and covenants *back*. This implies that we first took or got them at some point earlier.

Recommend—To enter the temple, we need a temple recommend. This comes from the Latin word meaning "to trust to."[28] With the prefix *re* it means "to trust to again." This implies that those going to the temple worthily have been trusted before.

Reconcile, reconciliation—This is one of the synonyms for the Greek word for "atonement."[29] It means to draw together or make friendly again.[30] To be reconciled with the Lord is to be brought back together with Him again and to be made His friend again.

Redeem, Redeemer, Redemption—These words comes to us

from Latin and means "to get" or "buy back."[31] We can understand that the Redeemer has "purchased" us from sin through the Atonement if we will repent and follow Him. This word, by indicating that the Savior is purchasing us *back*, also indicates that we were once His or the Father's before the Fall.

Religion—This is a Latin phrase meaning to "bind back."[32] "Binding," particularly of the brokenhearted, suggests entering into covenant with the Lord in order to heal a wound (Isaiah 61:1; D&C 35:24; D&C 43:9). Therefore, religion—true religion—is a binding back, or again, of the Lord's followers so that they can be healed. They bind themselves back, or again, to follow and serve Him.

Remember—One of the most important words in the gospel, *remember* means to bring back to mind.[33] We covenant to remember the Lord, to bring Him back to our minds continually (D&C 20:77, 79). In exchange, we are promised His Spirit.

One of the primary functions of the temple is to teach us the principle of remembrance. The garment is meant to be a constant reminder of the Lord, our nakedness without Him, our permanent spiritual and physical death without Him, our place before Him, and the covenants we have made with Him. The tokens, signs, and words mentioned by President Young also serve these same functions. We are taught by the principle of repetition as we return to the temple again and again on behalf of those who were not blessed to receive their endowment while alive. The more we repeat this process, the better we will remember the lessons and power of the endowment.

Renew—We take the sacrament to renew our covenants. This means, as you might guess, to make new again.[34] This is also one of the functions of the Atonement.

Repent—Also one of the most important words in the gospel, *repent* means to be penitent again. The Savior appropriately taught us that our repentance should function to make us like a little child (3 Nephi 9:22). Repentance may therefore be properly defined as regaining innocence before the Lord. (*See also* 3 Nephi 11: 37–38.)

Restitution—This word is properly associa
titution (i.e., atoning for our sins) or with *re*
us from Latin and means "to set up again."
priately describes the restoration of the L
the effects of the Lord's atonement (Acts

Restore—Much like *restitution*, this word ...
back."[36] We normally associate this word with the Lord's restored
gospel, but it also coincides with the Greek word for "atonement"
meaning a "restoration to the divine." Significantly, this word may
also suggest the Michael to Adam to Michael progression and
the Atonement itself. Those who are righteous in mortality will
be restored to righteousness in the eternities (Alma 41:12–15). By
practicing righteousness, we can be restored to a righteous and
godlike state.

Reveal, Revelation—From Latin, this word literally means to
"draw back the veil."[37] Revelation is therefore a drawing back of
the veil.

Revere, Reverence—This Latin word means "to fear again."[38]
The word *fear*, in a gospel context, is meant to represent a feeling
of sanctity, awe, and deep respect. This is a much more solemn
meaning than the fear that is the opposite of faith.

Following the translation of these common gospel words, we
find that the Lord's plan involves doing things again that perhaps
we don't remember doing in the first place. These very important
words that imply repetition—even though they may seem to be
happening for the first time—can only be understood and appre-
ciated with an eternal perspective. That eternal perspective can
only come from the temple, where past, present, and future—the
bookends of eternity—Michael to Adam to Michael—all come
together.

Summary

ü   Adam and Eve are our role models. We are to follow their pattern throughout our experience in the temple and throughout all of mortality.

ü   An understanding of the true meaning of the words associated with the endowment can change nearly everything about your temple experience.

ü   *Adam* means mankind. It refers to all of us, whether we're men or women.

ü   *Michael* means who is like God. It is the pre-mortal and post-mortal name of Adam. It represents mankind's origin and his potential destiny.

ü   When Adam (mankind) symbolically comes unto Christ, he begins his return to Michael (godliness or being like God). This is done through the ordinances and covenants of the gospel, particularly those in the temple.

ü   *Temple* means a palace. It also denotes a place where the horizontal meets the vertical. In other words, it is where man meets God and where man's will is brought in harmony with God's will.

ü   *Endowment* means both a gift and an act of clothing. Adam and Eve received both a gift and a clothing from the Lord before they were cast out of the Garden of Eden. Their clothing of animal skins came from the first sacrifice, which led directly to the first endowment in this sense of the word.

ü   A *token* is a person's individual proof of his agreement with another party. When the two parties' halves are "thrown together," the token is complete.

ü   Many important words in the Gospel of Jesus Christ begin with the prefix *re*, which means "back" or "again." Like the pattern of Michael, to Adam, and back to Michael, these words imply a return to a heavenly state. The temple gives us the eternal perspective to understand the full meaning and importance of these words.

Notes

1. For more on this subject, see the definition of *profane* in this section.
2. The words "covenant" and "ordinance" are the subject of their very own chapter, so don't fret over their absence in this introduction.
3. James Strong, *Strong's Exhaustive Concordance of the Bible*, Hebrew word 120.
4. Alonzo Gaskill, *The Savior and the Serpent*, 26–27.
5. Strong, *Strong's Exhaustive Concordance*, Hebrew word 4317.
6. Bruce R. McConkie, *Doctrines of the Restoration*, 84.
7. Strong, *Strong's Exhaustive Concordance*, Hebrew word 2332.
8. Joseph Fielding McConkie, *Gospel Symbolism*, 255–56.
9. *Webster's New World Dictionary of the American Language*, 1962 Ed.
10. Strong, *Strong's Exhaustive Concordance*, Greek word 1746.
11. *The Personal Writings of Joseph Smith*, Dean C. Jessee, ed., 105.
12. First Presidency Letter, 10 October 1988, emphasis added.
13. *Webster's New World Dictionary*, 1962 Ed.
14. *Webster's New World Dictionary*, 1962 Ed.
15. Strong, *Strong's Exhaustive Concordance*, Greek word 2643
16. Ibid.
17. Strong, *Strong's Exhaustive Concordance*, Hebrew word 3722.
18. Strong, *Strong's Exhaustive Concordance*, Hebrew word 1964.
19. Hugh Nibley, *Mormonism and Early Christianity*, 358.
20. Ibid.
21. *Webster's New World Dictionary*, 1962 Ed.

22. Todd Compton, "Symbolism," *Encyclopedia of Mormonism*, 1428
23. Ibid.
24. *Oxford English Dictionary*, 1989 ed.
25. Strong, *Strong's Exhaustive Concordance*, Hebrew word 226.
26. After you have gone through the temple, you may find it insightful to search the scriptures, particularly the Gospel of John, for other more specific references to signs that point to and identify Christ. In doing this, remember that *sign* and *token* are very closely related. For more discussion on signs and tokens, see the subsection on the Two Trees in Chapter 4
27. *Webster's New World Dictionary*, 1962 Ed.
28. Ibid.
29. Strong, *Strong's Exhaustive Concordance*, Greek word 2643.
30. *Webster's New World Dictionary*, 1962 Ed.
31. Ibid.
32. Ibid.
33. Ibid
34. Ibid
35. Ibid
36. Ibid
37. Ibid.
38. Ibid.

CHAPTER 3

A BRIEF OVERVIEW OF ADAM AND EVE

The first pieces of the puzzle are Adam and Eve. Elder Talmage's description of the endowment is the ideal starting point for any effort to understand the endowment and begin putting the pieces together.

> The Temple Endowment, as administered in modern temples, comprises instruction relating to the significance and sequence of past dispensations, and the importance of the present as the greatest and grandest era in human history. This course of instruction includes a recital of the most prominent events of the creative period, the condition of our first parents in the Garden of Eden, their disobedience and consequent expulsion from that blissful abode, their condition in the lone and dreary world when doomed to live by labor and sweat, the plan of redemption by which the great transgression may be atoned, the period of the great apostasy, the restoration of the Gospel with all its ancient powers and privileges, the absolute and indispensable condition of personal purity and devotion to the right in present life, and a strict compliance with Gospel requirements.[1]

This statement by Elder Talmage is only two sentences long, and they're obviously no ordinary sentences. They're full of great meaning, and we could write books on them. Without trying to write and digest all of those books at once, we can safely summarize these two sentences by stating that one of the functions of the temple endowment is to teach us the plan of salvation.

The endowment, like the plan of salvation that it teaches,

begins with the Creation and the story of our first parents, Adam and Eve. According to Elder Talmage, their journey included the following:

- the Creation
- Adam and Eve's condition in the first temple, the Garden of Eden
- their disobedience in eating the forbidden fruit
- their expulsion from the Garden of Eden and fall from the presence of God
- their works and trials in the world
- their return to the presence of God

Adam and Eve were placed in the Garden of Eden. In this state, they enjoyed, at times, the personal presence of God. They were godlike because of their heritage, being created in the exact image of God. They were also godlike in that they were pure and free from sin. But, this purity was very fragile and untested because they were not yet godlike in so many other ways. They had not learned to choose for themselves between good and evil (2 Nephi 2:26–27) and had not yet overcome the trials of the world. Like newborns, they were pure, but they were inexperienced and untested. In short, they were like God in some ways, but not like God in many very important ways.

The next chapter, the Fall, is the first step for Adam and Eve to becoming godlike through their actions. Their Fall is perhaps the most misunderstood event of human history. Many in the world view the Fall as a curse that brought all mankind into a world of sin. There is just enough truth in this view to corrupt and confuse millennia of human beings about the true meaning of the Fall. The temple places the Fall in its proper position as the inevitable next step in mankind's journey back to the presence of God and the opportunity to become godlike in every other way, as the Lord Himself commanded (Matthew 5:48). The temple teaches us that the victory claimed by Satan with the Fall is actually minuscule compared to the victory gained by the Lord.

After the Fall, Adam and Eve are cast into the world where

they have to work and sweat to survive. They no longer enjoy personal visits from the Lord. They are at some point blessed with children who prove to be a great source of both joy and heartache to them. If this experience sounds familiar, that's because it is our same experience on Earth today. This is the "earth" state mentioned by President Young that we must overcome to regain the presence of God. The temple teaches us the essential lessons that guide us through the heartache and trials of this world by giving us an eternal perspective of where we came from and where we can return. The temple also keeps us firmly planted through the good times by keeping us focused on what really matters in mortality and eternity.

The rest of the journey back to the Father and to being like Him is also set out in the endowment. According to Elder Talmage, that journey is marked by putting the Atonement into practice. Elder Talmage speaks specifically of many covenants that are made in the temple, so we can safely assume that those covenants are essential to make the journey back to the presence of God. If we call the path back to God a road, then covenants are the pavement and markers on that road. If we call the path back to God a ladder, then covenants are the rungs on the ladder. Making the covenants is essential, but covenants are only promises to act a certain way. Therefore, keeping those covenants is the real challenge.

In short, the temple takes mankind on the journey from Michael to Adam and back to Michael—from being with and like God, to being mortal on the Earth, to again being like God and with God.

Adam and Eve's Journey from Three Perspectives

As Elder Talmage notes, we are taught this journey back to the Father from the perspective of Adam and Eve. To learn from this journey, we must put ourselves in their shoes. They are not just characters in a story or even an example; they are our role models. We follow them because they perfectly represent our origin, our current state, and our final destination—if we successfully follow their examples. Understanding this point makes the puzzle pieces much easier to recognize and assemble.

In the scriptures, the Lord teaches Adam and Eve's journey, or the journey from Michael to Adam and back to Michael, in three different themes. By studying these themes, these puzzle pieces, we prepare ourselves much better to enter the temple and to learn the lessons that the Lord is trying to teach us in the endowment.

The Genesis, Moses, and Abraham Accounts—The first group of scriptural lessons about Adam and Eve and the plan of salvation is the familiar story found in Genesis, Moses, and Abraham. These accounts need no introduction. As long as we understand that we are to consider ourselves as Adam and Eve and understand their origin and destiny as children of God, studying these accounts will prepare us extremely well for our own endowment.

The Ancient Temple Accounts—The second group of scriptural accounts is the records of the Tabernacle and ancient temple of the Lord.[2] The book of Exodus reveals a surprising amount of detail about the ancient temple. Just like the current temple, the ancient temple experience was based on the story of Adam and Eve and their journey back to the Lord. In the ancient temple, the story of Adam and Eve was taught almost purely by the use of symbols. We will examine those symbols in order to understand the lessons from the ancient temple about the plan of salvation.

Many scholars, both in and outside of the Church, have devoted their lives to studying the ancient temple. The volume and depth of their writings are staggering and can be overwhelming to someone wanting to learn from these scholars. However, an understanding of the ancient temple should *not* be restricted to scholarly circles and people with a title or initials adorning their names. There is too much to be learned from the ancient temple for it to be understood by so few. A basic understanding of the ancient temple will work wonders in preparing Latter-day Saints to enter and reenter the temple. This book will seek to help you gain such an understanding.

Other Scriptural Accounts Taught with Symbolism—The third type of scriptural account of the journey from Michael to Adam back to Michael is found scattered in various places throughout the scriptures. This third type of account takes some level of understanding of symbolism to recognize and apply. We're just getting used to understanding Adam and Eve as our exemplars, but they are actually not the only examples of the journey from pre-mortal to mortal to Godlike in the scriptures. Likewise, the Garden of Eden and the ancient Tabernacle and temple are not the only temples found in the scriptures. Temple experiences are also depicted through many other people and events in the scriptures.

Since the Lord uses symbolism as his main method of teaching in the temple, we will briefly study some examples of gospel symbolism that teach us to identify and understand many other lessons of temples and temple experiences throughout the scriptures. If you recognize a particular passage in the scriptures as a temple experience, you will understand your own temple experience better.

These scriptural temple experiences often occur on mountains. The LDS Bible Dictionary states that mountains can serve as temples "in cases of extreme poverty or emergency." To me, this is an understatement. I have yet to find a scriptural account involving a mountain that is not a templelike experience. As I see it, the words "temple" and "mountain" are almost perfectly interchangeable in the scriptures. Mountains are literally where heaven meets Earth. They are literally the closest place to heaven on Earth. An altar expresses this same principle on a smaller scale. The symbolism is clear and unmistakable. As a general rule, any time you see a reference to a mountain in the scriptures, you may assume that it is referring to a temple. Whatever the experience is that is depicted on that mountain, you may generally assume that is a temple experience.

These experiences may include man meeting God (Exodus

3, 20, 34; Ether 3), man receiving specific instruction from God (Moses 1; 1 Nephi 17; Exodus 3; 20), man finding refuge from the world (Genesis 19; Joel 2), or God's true nature being revealed to man (Matthew 17; Mark 9). Notably, the examples also include the most direct similitude of the sacrifice of the Lord Jesus Christ: Abraham's sacrifice of his son Isaac (Genesis 22). These are all temple experiences, even though they don't occur in a building specifically called a temple. They are too sacred to occur any place but a temple.

More important, they are all temple experiences because they show man being redeemed from the Fall (Ether 3:13) and actually seeing God. The temple is where we receive the blessings that fully redeem us from the Fall and allow us to see Him.

The temple is our own place to receive instruction from the Lord, to find refuge from the world, and even one day to be redeemed from the Fall and see the Lord. It is, again, the key to putting the Atonement into full practice in our lives. Recognizing these kinds of experiences in the scriptures as temple experiences broadens our understanding of such temple blessings in our own lives.

SUMMARY

- The temple teaches us by relating the story of Adam and Eve. We need to look at Adam and Eve as patterns for our own lives. In this way, the temple marches us from one end of eternity to the other.
- To help us understand the temple better, the Lord has given us three groups of accounts of the Adam and Eve story and the plan of salvation.
- Generally speaking, mountains represent temples in the scriptures. Any time you see a reference to something happening on a mountain in the scriptures, you may generally assume it is a temple experience of some sort.
- Temple experiences in the scriptures also include accounts

of people seeing or meeting the Lord. These experiences are so sacred that they can be interpreted as temple experiences whether or not they occurred in an actual temple.

Notes
1. James E. Talmage, *The House of the Lord*, 83.
2. I am using the term "ancient temple" to refer to both the Tabernacle and the temple in Jerusalem (Solomon's temple, Zerubbabel's temple, and Herod's temple). Most of the ancient temple references will be to the Tabernacle. While the Tabernacle is not specifically called a temple, it was, in fact, a temple, and the scriptures teach us much more about the Tabernacle than the Jerusalem temple.

Chapter 4

Adam and Eve's Journey According to Genesis, Moses, and Abraham

The Moses and Abraham accounts of Adam and Eve give us a glimpse of what happened even before the Creation. These glimpses are worth noting because they lay some foundation that helps put the rest of the Garden of Eden accounts and all of the other pieces of the puzzle in perspective.

The Moses Account

Moses 4:1–4 recounts the war in Heaven, where Satan presented his plan and the Savior volunteered to fulfill the Father's plan. This account is tucked in the middle of Adam and Eve's experience in the Garden of Eden.

> And I, the Lord God, spake unto Moses saying: That Satan, whom thou hast commanded in the name of my Only Begotten, is the same which was from the beginning, and he came before me, saying—Behold, here am I, send me, I will be thy son, and I will redeem all mankind, that one should shall not be lost, and surely I will do it; wherefore give me thine honor.
>
> But, behold, my Beloved Son, which was my Beloved and

Chosen from the beginning, said unto me—Father, thy will be done, and the glory be thine forever.

Wherefore, because that Satan rebelled against me, and sought to destroy the agency of man, which I, the Lord God, had given him, and also, that I should give unto him mine own power; by the power of mine Only Begotten, I caused that he should be cast down;

And he became Satan, yea, even the devil, the father of all lies, to deceive and to blind men, and to lead them captive at his will, even as many as would not hearken unto my voice.

This scripture reveals quite a bit about the nature of Satan. He personifies the "hell" that President Young noted we must overcome. Notice how many times he speaks the words "I" and "me." We can tell right off that these are among his favorite words. His selfishness is a major part of what drives him to be the eternal enemy of the Savior.

By contrast, notice the Savior's vocabulary. He never uses the words *I* or *me*. His entire focus is on fulfilling the will of the Father and glorifying the Father.

Satan can be expected to oppose the Lord at every possible turn. He will stop at nothing to lie, to deceive, and to lead away as many as he possibly can. He is infinitely more vicious and vile than anyone we could ever meet in the flesh. He will forever be insanely jealous of the Savior, whose plan was accepted over his in the pre-mortal life. This jealousy is the cause of his undying and unquenchable desire to make us miserable and lead us away from the Savior. Make no mistake about it. As we put ourselves in the shoes of Adam and Eve, our best defense is to avoid him altogether. He has as much power over us as we give him, but no more than that.

The Moses account also tells us of the exhausting revelation in which Moses saw the expanse and infinity of God's creations (Moses 1). In this revelation, the Lord taught Moses about "the earth upon which" he stood (Moses 1:40) and "the first man of all men" called Adam (Moses 1:34). This vision sapped all of Moses' power and left him limp and powerless for many hours (Moses 1:9–10). After beholding and attempting to comprehend the incomprehensible, Moses declared, "Now, for this cause I know that man is nothing, which thing I never had supposed" (Moses 1:10).

According to Elder Talmage's quote, the endowment in the modern temple teaches us the same thing. However, at some risk, and with the benefit of the rest of Moses 1, I am respectfully going to disagree with the great prophet Moses about his conclusion that "man is nothing." I acknowledge that a single man is microscopic among the Lord's endless creations. But consider the power of verse 39, where we learn that the Lord's work and glory is to bring to pass the immortality and eternal life of man, as microscopic as he may be by himself. The message I get from Moses' vision and this quote is that man is *everything*.

The Lord's creations are infinite, and it is certainly easy for man to lose track of a mere one man among infinity. However, the mere one is the very focus and purpose of infinity's existence. All of the creations that Moses saw were created just for man. God's own mission is to glorify man. Man is the direct subject of the Lord's work and glory. Man must, therefore, be infinitely more than nothing. With God's help, man can be everything. If this were not true, then the Lord's work and glory would be in vain.

Keep this in mind as you enter the temple. Everything laid out in the temple is done for you, as a child of God. You are the one the Savior wants to ransom from the grip of Satan. You are the one the Lord seeks to make immortal and eternal. You are the reason for the Creation. It's not done for you alone, but it is, nevertheless, for you.

THE ABRAHAM ACCOUNT

The Abraham account also teaches us some of what happened before the Creation. Abraham teaches us that intelligences "were organized before the world was; and among all these were many of the noble and great ones" (Abraham 3:22). The Father chose

His rulers from these "noble and great" spirits. The Abraham account identifies the greatest of these greats as the Savior (Abraham 3:24). This knowledge—that the Father chose the Savior and other great people to map out His plan on Earth before the Creation—helps put mortality and the temple experience in perspective.

The Abraham account also introduces a phrase that we hear throughout the scriptures. In giving its own brief account of the war in heaven, Abraham 3:26 refers to those who chose to follow the Savior as those who kept "their first estate." The same verse also teaches us that if we keep our "second estate" (mortality), we will "have glory added upon" us "for ever and ever" (Abraham 3:26). This scripture lays a perfect backdrop for understanding mortality. We are here because we kept our first estate. If we keep our second estate, through the covenants and ordinances of the temple, we will receive eternal glory. We can take courage in knowing that we have already kept our first estate, so the goal is well within our reach.

THE GENESIS ACCOUNT

Created in the Image of God—The first chapter of Genesis describes the most important product of the Creation: mankind.

> And God said, Let us make man in our image, after our likeness: and let them have dominion over the fish of the sea, and over the fowl of the air, and over the cattle, and over all the earth, and over every creeping thing that creepeth upon the earth.
>
> So God created man in his own image, in the image of God created he him; male and female created he them (Genesis 1:26–27).

The operative word in this section is the Hebrew verb *tsalam*. It is the core of the verbal expression "to create in one's own image." It means exactly what it says and more. *Tsalam* in modern Hebrew is used to mean "photocopy." The word means, as clearly as it is possible to express, to create an exact duplicate of something. So when Genesis, Moses, and Abraham speak of God creating man in God's own image, it is as literal as can be (Genesis 1:26–27). This is one of the first lessons of man's divine Godlike origin. Man is not a graduate of primordial ooze, but is created in the express image of his Father.

Placement in the Garden of Eden—After Adam and Eve were formed, they were placed in the Garden of Eden. The Garden of Eden was the first temple on Earth.[1] The Garden of Eden is not the same place as Eden alone. All three accounts place the Garden at the east of Eden, so it's a part of Eden, but they are not synonymous. As the east is the holy direction, the Garden of Eden is set aside as a holy place within Eden, just like a temple.

THE TWO TREES

Two trees are specifically mentioned in the Garden of Eden: The tree of life and the tree of knowledge of good and evil. The tree of life also appears at the other end of the Bible, in Revelation, as the goal and final destination of the twelve tribes of gathered Israel (Revelation 22:2). If the tree of life in Lehi's vision represented the love of God, then the tree of life in the Garden represents a fullness of that love. Unlike the tree in Lehi's vision, nobody is ashamed of eating from the tree of life in the Garden of Eden. Likewise, nobody is seen falling away after eating from the tree of life, unlike the tree in Lehi's vision (1 Nephi 8:25). The tree of life in the Garden of Eden has an eternal impact.

The tree of life in the Garden of Eden represents the presence of God.[2] This is not just a sample of His love; this is His actual presence.

On the other hand, the tree of knowledge of good and evil typifies mortality. This tree has all the characteristics of mortality itself. Eating from it ushered in mortality for Adam, Eve, and all of us who followed them to Earth (2 Nephi 2:23). Mortality is right at the middle of our eternal journey, just as the tree was in the middle of the Garden of Eden. A knowledge of good and evil is the central point of mortality. It is the opposition that is essential to our growth (2 Nephi 2:11). Just like mortality, eating from this tree brings us misery, but it also brings us joy (2 Nephi 2:23). In mortality, we are certain to sin, but we are given the opportunity to repent and overcome sin (2 Nephi 2:21). Mortality gives us the opportunity to learn and grow for ourselves by choosing the good from the evil (2 Nephi 2:26–27). As unpleasant as this tree might be at times, there is no substitute for it and no way around it if we are to become like God.

Just as the tree of knowledge of good and evil was in the midst of the Garden, the Savior came in the meridian of time to redeem us from the Fall (Moses 5:57; 6:57). The tree of knowledge of good and evil marked the beginning of mortality, and the Savior came in the middle of mortality (the meridian of time) to allow mankind to return to the tree of life. Christ is in the middle of this and every other lesson about the temple.

We know that Adam was told not to eat of the tree of knowledge of good and evil in the Garden of Eden, but there was no such restriction on the tree of life (Moses 3:17). In fact, the Lord specifically allowed Adam to eat freely from any tree *except* for the tree of knowledge of good and evil (Moses 3:16). The Genesis and Moses accounts don't even mention the tree of life until *after* Adam and Eve have eaten the fruit of the tree of knowledge of good and evil.

Eating from the tree of life and enjoying the presence of the Lord was perfectly acceptable before the Fall, but this changed as a result of the Fall. The Lord set cherubim and a flaming sword to guard the tree of life after the Fall so that Adam and Eve wouldn't live forever in their sins. After the Fall, they were not worthy of the full presence of God (Moses 4:31).[3] They would have been "found unclean before the judgment-seat of God; and no unclean thing can dwell with God" (1 Nephi 10:21). They would have been cast out forever.

In other words, if they had eaten of the tree of life—if they had been symbolically brought back to the full presence of God—their judgment day would have arrived too soon, before they had repented. They would have had no chance to repent, to grow, and to regain their innocence before God (Alma 42:4–5). The cherubim and flaming sword were not placed there to punish or dismember Adam and Eve, but to *protect* them from eating of the tree of life too soon.

We want to eat from the tree of life! We should want it more than anything else. It represents the presence of God. Because we want to get there, the cherubim with the flaming sword are not our enemies any more than they were Adam and Eve's enemies. In our vocabulary chapter, we learned that cherubim represent sentinels, a word we recognize from the Prophet Brigham Young's definition of the endowment. We look forward to meeting and passing these sentinels, as long as we are prepared.

A flaming sword conjures up images of painful burning and cutting, but that's not the point. The sword isn't there to dismember us or scare us off; it's there for our protection. Again, we look forward to approaching this sword as long as we're prepared for it.

To paraphrase President Young, the endowment exists to prepare us to pass the cherubim and flaming sword. According to President Young, we need certain words, signs, and tokens in order to get back to the tree of life.[4] Remember from our definitions chapter that tokens are our proof of covenants, and signs are very closely related to them. The lesson here is that we need covenants to get back to the presence of God.

Despite what some people might take from President Young's description of the endowment, there are no magical words or gestures that will, by themselves, make us worthy to get back to the presence of God. Becoming worthy of the tree of life is not about solving riddles or memorizing things; it is about making and keeping sacred covenants. According to President Young, the words, signs, and tokens pertain to the "Holy Priesthood." Therefore, they are all symbolic in one way or another of temple covenants made and kept.

In some ways, receiving these words, signs, and tokens is like receiving a temple recommend. A recommend will allow us to enter the temple, but there is much more to a recommend than that. The recommend is an emblem or culmination of our preparation and worthiness, but it does not make us worthy. We don't simply "get" a recommend. In order to obtain a recommend, we have to meet standards of worthiness. We have to obtain a burning testimony. We have to love the Lord thoroughly. A recommend is not just a piece of paper—it's a symbol of a life of worthiness.

Once we obtain a recommend, it does us little good if we don't actually use it. We need to return frequently and make the temple a central part of our lives. Again, it's not just a piece of paper; it's a commitment to continuing worthiness and blessings.

The temple recommend is a symbol of everything that went into obtaining it and everything that flows from it. So it is with the words, signs, and tokens mentioned by President Young. They embody everything that goes into them and every blessing that follows them. They are symbolic of a special relationship between the two parties to the covenants, but they don't replace the covenants that they represent. If we do not learn this lesson, we're missing the point.

On this subject, Elder Marion D. Hanks stated:

> What really matters is the kind of people we are, the kind of people we become as we return to the temple to serve others and to ponder our own progress in the principles that were critical in this life—to learn and do the will of the Father, to serve and share, to love and mercifully give and forgive, to be loyal, to be clean and pure, to give to his work whatever we are privileged to give. In short, the mature experience of temple worship ideally has the power to produce—and sometimes does—a new different kind of person who knows the path of principles followed by the Savior and gives them application in his or her personal life.[5]

It's not just *knowing* something that gets us back to the Lord; it's *applying* what we learn from all the covenants and ordinances of the temple. This process of applying the lessons is what makes us more like God.

THE TEMPLE GIVES US A GLIMPSE OF THE ETERNITY WITHOUT HAVING TO DIE FIRST

Mortality must be experienced in order to be understood. There is no substitute for mortality in the plan of salvation.

You would think that the same would hold true for immortality. It would make sense that we would have to die in order to understand what awaits us when we die. Well, the temple makes it possible for us to get a glimpse of immortality and learn important lessons about it without having to experience it. In other words, through the temple, we don't have to die to get a glimpse of the other side of the veil.

If we want to enter the celestial kingdom, we must finish mortality. That means we must die. After we have finished mortality, we will die, and we will find ourselves wanting to eat of the tree of life and enter the presence of God. We can expect to find guardians like the cherubim and flaming sword guarding that tree of life. We will find ourselves in sore need of the signs, tokens, and words mentioned by President Young to pass these guardians. This is an experience that normally we would ordinarily and quite honestly have to die for.

While we have to come to Earth to experience mortality, we do not have to die to experience a taste of heaven. The temple can give us that same taste. We have to live in order to prepare ourselves for the tree of life, but the temple takes away our need to die in order to get a glimpse of the tree of life. Moreover, when we do die, we can have the advantage of knowing how to get to the tree of life without guessing or hoping that we already did the right thing (read: received and kept the necessary covenants and ordinances) to get to the tree of life. The temple teaches us what we need to *know*, to *do*, and to *have* on the other side of the veil.

Not only does the temple give us a glimpse of post-mortal life without having to die, the temple also gives us a glimpse of our *pre*-mortal life as well. By helping us understand where we came from, the temple better teaches us to understand where we can go.

No other experience can prepare us for, or take us to, the other side of mortality like the temple. The temple lays out the plan of salvation from the beginning to the end. The Plan teaches us where we came from, who we are, where we are, where we need to go, and how to get there.

Adam and Eve were *not* banished from the Garden to be forever cut off from the presence of God. In fact, it's quite the opposite. They were destined to get back to their heavenly home. They had eaten from the tree of life before the Fall and their goal was to get back to that tree. The Lord gave them instructions, a gift, and clothing to help them navigate their way through their experience after eating the fruit of the tree of knowledge of good and evil and eventually return to the tree of life. The plan of salvation is this same journey through mortality back to the presence of God. The keys that we need to make it back to our heavenly home are given in the covenants and ordinances of the temple.

SUMMARY

- Adam and Eve's experience in the Garden of Eden teaches us the plan of salvation through symbols.
- The Garden of Eden was the first temple on Earth.
- The tree of life represents the presence of God or the celestial kingdom. We want to eat of this fruit but we have to be worthy and cleansed from sin. If Adam and Eve had eaten of the fruit before they had a chance to repent, they would have been cast out because they were still in sin and had not yet repented. Their day of judgment would have come too soon.
- The tree of knowledge of good and evil typifies mortality and our experience on Earth. Adam and Eve's eating of this tree began mortality for them and for all of us. In the middle of this mortality, or the meridian of time, Christ came to offer the Atonement, so that we could return and eat from the tree of life.

- The cherubim and flaming sword that guard the tree of life are not our enemies. The endowment gives us the words, signs, and tokens to enable us to pass these guardians and return to the tree of life.
- These words, signs, and tokens all relate to ordinances and covenants of the temple. They don't represent shortcuts or answers to riddles; they represent temple covenants that we must make and keep.
- The temple takes us from one end of the plan of salvation to the other. It teaches us, through the example of Adam and Eve, where we came from, who we are, where we need to go, and how to get there. These are the greatest lessons we can learn in life.

Notes

1. Donald W. Parry, "Garden of Eden: Prototype Sanctuary," *Temples of the Ancient World*, 126–51.
2. "The Tree of Life in Ancient Cultures," C. Wilfred Griggs, *Ensign*, June, 1988.
3. To be clear, Adam and Eve did have an interim period of contact with the Lord after they had eaten of the forbidden fruit, but before they were cast out of the Garden. During that period, the Lord visited them to teach them how to return to Him.
4. Brigham Young, *Discourses of Brigham Young*, 416.
5. Marion D. Hanks, "Christ Manifested to His People," *Temples of the Ancient World*, 24.

CHAPTER 5

ADAM AND EVE AND THE PLAN OF SALVATION IN THE ANCIENT TEMPLE

Joseph Smith taught that, "The order of the house of God has been, and ever will be, the same, even after Christ comes."[1] With this in mind, it should not be surprising that the ancient temple followed the same pattern noted by Elder Talmage. Like the temple of the restored Gospel, the ancient temple also taught the progression of Adam and Eve from the Fall back to the presence of God, as represented by the Holy of Holies.

However, the ancient temple tells this story entirely by the use of symbols. Symbolism also sets the landscape of the modern temple experience. To understand the symbolism of the temple is to understand the shapes of the puzzle pieces and to put them together one by one.

The term "ancient temple" is meant to include the Tabernacle and the temple at Jerusalem. The Tabernacle was basically a portable temple for the Israelites while they were still wandering in the wilderness, before they were able to make their permanent home in the promised land. The term "Jerusalem temple" is used to include Solomon's temple, the temple that was later restored and known as the Zerubbabel temple, and Herod's temple, which stood in Jerusalem in the Savior's day.

THE LAW OF MOSES AND THE AARONIC PRIESTHOOD

Of these ancient temples, the scriptures give the most detail about the Tabernacle. Moses and Aaron were the principal figures of the Tabernacle. The Lord's choice of Moses and Aaron as the main people associated with the Tabernacle is no coincidence. The Mosaic law was named after Moses, and the Aaronic Priesthood is named after Aaron. As we will see, both the Mosaic law and the Aaronic Priesthood play a prominent role in understanding the temple.

The law of Moses was given as a schoolmaster to bring the people to Christ (Galatians 3:24). It prepared people for His coming. The rites of the Mosaic law, particularly the sacrifices, were specifically designed to typify Christ and point the people to His coming. When Christ came, He fulfilled the Mosaic law (Matthew 5:17). He did not abolish the law; he added to it with teachings that took the people closer to Heaven. The law of Moses pointed people to Christ, and Christ delivers people to the Father (John 17:3).

The same kind of preparation and delivery is served by the priesthood that is named for Moses' companion in the Tabernacle, Aaron. The Aaronic Priesthood is sometimes called the preparatory priesthood. Just as the Mosaic law led to Christ, the Aaronic Priesthood leads to the Melchizedek Priesthood. The Melchizedek Priesthood represents Christ, as it was originally called the Holy Priesthood, after the Order of the Son of God (D&C 107:3). Both the Mosaic law and the Aaronic Priesthood lead directly to, and are fulfilled by, the Son of God.

The Mosaic law did not have the power to bring people back to the presence of God, but that wasn't its purpose. Its purpose was to bring people to Christ. It is Christ who has the power to save and to bring His people back to the presence of God. Bringing people to the promised land (the presence of God the Father, the tree of life, or the highest degree of the celestial kingdom) is Christ's role and power.[2]

The perfect illustration of this lesson is the Exodus story. Moses led the Israelites out of bondage, through the waters of the

Red Sea (symbolic of the ordinance of baptism, which is administered by the Aaronic Priesthood), and through the wilderness. However, Moses never got to lead the Israelites into the promised land. It wasn't his role. That honor was held by Joshua, who was a direct representation of Christ. His actual name, before we anglicize it into our own language, was Yehoshua. You may recognize this as the same name as Jesus. For some reason, the name Yehoshua came to us as "Joshua" from the Old Testament Hebrew language and "Jesus" from the Greek New Testament translation. Joshua is a very literal representation of Jesus, and it was he who delivered the Israelites to the symbolic presence of the Father in the promised land.

Likewise, the ordinances of the Aaronic Priesthood, such as baptism, have the power to bring people to Christ and to membership in His church. However, they do not have the power to bring exaltation or entry into the promised land of the celestial kingdom. That power is held by the Melchizedek Priesthood in the higher ordinances of the temple.

The Aaronic Priesthood and the Mosaic law are both indispensable in the temple and the plan of salvation. After all, there would be no access to the ordinances of the temple without baptism and the Aaronic Priesthood first. Their roles are different, however, and that difference, like everything else, points to Christ.

The roles played by Moses and Aaron in the ancient temple still carry profound symbolic lessons in the temple of this dispensation. They take us to the Son of God, and the Savior takes us to the presence of the Father.

THE THREE AREAS OF THE TABERNACLE

The Tabernacle was divided into three main areas: An outer courtyard, the Holy Place, and the Holy of Holies. Many people were permitted to enter the outer courtyard, but few were allowed to enter the Holy Place. Only one person, the High Priest, was allowed to enter the Holy of Holies, and even that was only permitted once a year on the Day of Atonement.

These areas are symbolic of the telestial, terrestrial, and celestial kingdoms.[3] Like before, this division of three areas represents Adam and Eve's plight in the Garden of Eden. They were driven out of the Garden, away from the tree of life or the Holy of Holies, and into a mortal world that represents the telestial kingdom. Their goal was to return to the tree of life, which is represented by the Holy of Holies. To put the Atonement into practice is to reverse the effects of the Fall and travel from the outer courtyard (the telestial kingdom) and eventually back to the presence of God (the Holy of Holies).

ALTAR OF SACRIFICE

The first thing that greeted people who entered the outer courtyard of the Tabernacle was the altar of sacrifice. This was the spot where the Israelites offered animal sacrifices each day in similitude of the Atonement. This emphasizes the importance of the principle of sacrifice. Like just about everything else we have discussed, it points to Christ and His sacrifice. As it is the first article in the Tabernacle court, it is the foundation of everything that follows in the Tabernacle.

The principle of obedience is inseparable from the principle of sacrifice. The instructions for offering these sacrifices were very specific and had to be followed to the last detail (See Exodus 29:1–2). This is a lesson in exact obedience, which governs and also involves sacrifice. Renowned biblical scholar Jacob Neusner teaches that the rules for offering these sacrifices were so precise that they required the priest to offer the sacrifice with his right hand and receive the blood from the sacrificed animal with a cup in his left hand.[4] Another scholar believes that it was the opposite: The sacrifice was made with the left hand, and the blood was collected in the right hand.[5] Personally, I believe both scholars are probably correct. Regardless, the important thing is not to debate which hand received the blood of the sacrifice—the important thing is for us to receive the blood of the Lamb of God in our own lives and walk in the light of obedience so that His blood will cleanse us from all sin (1 John 1:7).

This lesson of sacrifice and obedience was taught to Adam immediately after he and Eve were driven out of the Garden.

> And he gave unto them commandments, that they should worship the Lord their God, and should offer the firstlings of their flocks, for an offering unto the Lord. And Adam was obedient unto the commandments of the Lord.
>
> And after many days an angel of the Lord appeared unto Adam, saying: Why dost thou offer sacrifices unto the Lord? And Adam said unto him: I know not, save the lord commanded me.
>
> And then the angel spake, saying: This thing is a similitude of the sacrifice of the Only Begotten of the Father, which is full of grace and truth.
>
> Wherefore, thou shalt do all that thou doest in the name of the Son, and thou shalt repent and call upon God in the name of the Son forevermore (Moses 5:5–8).

From this scripture, and from the specific instructions for the sacrifices at the Tabernacle, we see that sacrifice and obedience are no good without each other. All of our obedience in mortality will still not erase our sins. We need to receive the Atonement, the great and last sacrifice, to cleanse us (Alma 34:10). Likewise, we only enjoy the full blessings of the Atonement if we obey the Lord's commandments. We receive the blessings of the great sacrifice (represented by the blood shed with one hand of the priest and received with the other hand) through our obedience.

In the Tabernacle, all the sacrifices served to teach about and point to the Atonement. The sacrifice we are commanded to offer today also points to the Atonement, but it is not the sacrifice of an animal. Our sacrifice today is a broken heart and a contrite spirit (3 Nephi 9:19–20). This sacrifice represents complete submission to the Lord—a willingness to follow Christ at all costs. If we offer this basic sacrifice of a broken or willing heart and a contrite or deeply moved spirit, then we will be prepared to make any other sacrifice and keep any other commandment we may receive from the Lord. If we truly have a broken heart and contrite spirit, we will recognize our place in the fallen world and will do whatever the Lord asks to get back to the tree of life. Therefore, sacrifice and obedience are the foundation for all the other covenants of the temple.

THE LAVER AND WASHING AND ANOINTING

The next object in the outer courtyard was called the laver. It was a basin for washing. Its purpose is explained in Exodus 29, where the Lord gives instructions to prepare the priests to enter the Tabernacle (See also Exodus 30:19–20). The priests were to be washed with water from the laver (Exodus 29:4), anointed with oil (Exodus 29:7), and dressed in priestly robes (Exodus 29:5–6).[6] The ordinance of washing and anointing was part of the ancient temple, and it was revealed as part of the latter-day temple in Section 124 of the Doctrine and Covenants (D&C 124:39).

What is the purpose of washing with water and anointing with oil?

Washing—Water obviously represents cleansing. That much is clear by the very term "washing."

Anointing—Oil requires a little more explanation. In biblical times, anointing with olive oil was the practice or ritual associated with setting apart prophets, priests, and kings (Exodus 28:41; 1 Samuel 10:1; 1 Kings 19:16; Acts 10:38; Isaiah 61:1). This practice of anointing with oil also points to Christ. Both "Christ" and "Messiah" mean "anointed" or "anointed one" in Greek and Hebrew. He was anointed and chosen (Isaiah 61:1; Luke 4:18, 21).

Olive oil, which was used for the anointing, is a scriptural symbol for the Holy Ghost.[7] In the parable of the ten virgins, the five who had their lamps filled with oil symbolically had their lives filled with the Holy Ghost (D&C 45:56–57).

By understanding that oil represents the Holy Ghost, we can

see that the use of water and oil in washing and anointing gives us a familiar combination of water and the Spirit.

> Jesus answered and said unto him, Verily, verily, I say unto thee, Except a man be born again, he cannot see the kingdom of God.
>
> Nicodemus saith unto him, How can a man be born when he is old? can he enter the second time into his mother's womb, and be born?
>
> Jesus answered, Verily, verily, I say unto thee, Except a man be born of water and of the Spirit, he cannot enter into the kingdom of God (John 3:3–5).

This scripture is frequently quoted as a lesson on baptism and the gift of the Holy Ghost. But did you notice that the word "baptism" doesn't appear in the scripture? One reason for this might be that this scripture applies to more than just baptism and the Gift of the Holy Ghost. In the ordinances of washing and anointing, we see that there is more than one birth of water and the Spirit that is essential to our exaltation.

The sacrament may also be considered another symbolic birth of water and the Spirit. We take of the bread, representing the body of the Savior, and the water, representing the blood of the Savior. In return, we are promised His spirit (D&C 20:77, 79).

We are familiar with the ordinances of baptism and the sacrament since we experience them regularly. Because we're familiar with them, we don't see anything unusual or foreign about them. There is no reason not to be likewise familiar with the ordinances of washing and anointing, even though they should only be discussed in detail within the temple. They are another birth of water and the Spirit that is essential to our return to the presence of God.

This is another example of the purpose of the Aaronic Priesthood. Baptism, an ordinance of the Aaronic Priesthood, brings us into the Lord's Church. Baptism may be referred to as the covenant of salvation.

Washing and anointing are ordinances of the Melchizedek Priesthood that bring us into the Lord's house. The ordinances of the temple, carried through to the ordinance of celestial marriage, may be referred to as the covenant of exaltation.

The sacrament renews our covenants and helps us to be born again each time we take it. Baptism, washing and anointing, and the sacrament are all symbolic births of water and the Spirit. They are essential to entering the eternal kingdom of God. The ordinances of washing and anointing are another step on the symbolic journey from the outer courtyard (representing the telestial kingdom) back to the Holy of Holies (the celestial kingdom, the tree of life, or the presence of God).

If you've ever had the chance to read a dedicatory prayer for a temple, it may help you understand the ordinance of washing and anointing better. Temple dedicatory prayers tend to be very specific. President Kimball's prayer (rededicatory prayer, actually) for the Mesa temple specifically dedicates the windows, the furnishings, the dynamos, the heating and cooling systems, and all the other details that we take for granted.[8] Every last part of the temple is dedicated to perform its proper function. Understanding that our bodies are temples (1 Corinthians 3:16; D&C 93:35), it may be helpful to think of the ordinance of washing and anointing as a type of dedicatory prayer on our own temple.

THE HOLY PLACE

Moving from the outer courtyard, the holy place was a more select and sacred place. It represented the terrestrial kingdom. We don't know much about the specific things that the priests did inside the holy place because such sacred things were not meant to be discussed openly. The guidelines of respect for the sanctity of temple ordinances that govern the temple today are nothing new; they applied to the ancient temple as well. However, we clearly see more symbolic representations of Christ and the Atonement in the holy place. More specifically, we learn principles that are central to the gospel and our return to the tree of life.

The Menorah—On the left, inside the holy place, was a sacred lampstand or menorah. This lampstand contained seven branches that always burned. It is said to have resembled a tree, even the tree of life. It represents the Light of the World, who is Christ.

The Table of Shewbread and Wine—On the opposite side was the table of shewbread. This table contained bread and wine, which were laid out each Sabbath. This is an obvious symbol of the sacrament that we take each Sabbath. On one side of the holy place is the light that burns from olive oil. Again, olive oil represents the Holy Ghost. On the other side of the holy place are bread and wine, the emblems of the sacrament. Here we have yet another birth of water and the Spirit paving the way to return to the Lord.[9] The emblems on the right side of the holy place (the sacrament) lead to the emblem on the left (the Spirit). The Israelites read from right to left, so moving from right to left would have made sense to them.

Like the shadow by day and the pillar by night that guided the Israelites through the wilderness, the light of the lampstand is meant to guide us each day through our lives. Like the manna that came from heaven (Exodus 16) and the water that came from the rock on Mount Horeb (Exodus 17), the bread and wine are also meant to nourish us on each day of our journey to the tree of life.

The Altar of Incense—The final article in the holy place was the altar in front of the veil (Exodus 30). Incense was burned in it. Incense gives a unique flame and pillar of smoke that rises directly and narrowly and doesn't billow like other fires. This represents prayer that occurs directly before the veil that separates man from the Holy of Holies (Revelation 8:4). This is no ordinary prayer, however. This prayer is very close to the presence of God and is separated from Him only by the veil of fabric. To offer a prayer this close to the presence of God carries an exceptional power. This magnitude of prayer is illustrated in Section 88 of the Doctrine of Covenants where the Lord states, "Draw near unto me and I will draw near unto you; seek me diligently and ye shall find me; ask, and ye shall receive; knock and it shall be opened unto you" (D&C 88:63).

Moving from the outer courtyard to the holy place, we see all three principles taught to Adam when the angel appeared to him after the Fall: sacrifice, obedience, and prayer (Moses 5:5–8). Just as sacrifice (specifically, of a broken heart and contrite spirit) is the first principle that prepares us to accept any other commandment and sacrifice the Lord may ask, the principle of prayer gives us a very special communion with God that prepares us to enter His presence.

THE HOLY OF HOLIES

The Holy of Holies represented the presence of God, the celestial kingdom, and the tree of life. This is our ultimate goal. This is the final stop on the road from Michael, to Adam, through the Son of God, and back to Michael. We progress toward the Holy of Holies from the outer courtyard, or telestial kingdom, and through the holy place, or terrestrial kingdom. We progress from one kingdom to another by living the principles of sacrifice, obedience, and prayer and by a series of covenants and rebirths of water and the Spirit.

Separating the holy place from the Holy of Holies was a veil with cherubim woven into it (Exodus 26:31). The role of cherubim in guarding the Holy of Holies is something we have discussed much by now, but we will take time once again to remember the words of President Young on the endowment:

> Your endowment is, to receive all those ordinances in the House of the Lord, which are necessary for you, after you have departed this life, to enable you to walk back to the presence of the Father, passing the angels who stand as sentinels, being enabled to give them the key words, the signs and tokens, pertaining to the Holy Priesthood, and gain your eternal exaltation in spite of earth and hell.[10]

Again, these sentinels are our friends, not our enemies. We should not fear them as long as we are prepared, and the temple is where we learn and make those preparations.

The veil of the temple also points to the Atonement of Christ. After Christ completed the Atonement on the cross at Calvary, "the veil of the temple was rent in twain from the top to the bottom" (Matthew 27:51).[11] Once the portion of the Atonement that paid for our sins was complete, the veil was torn, cut right up the middle. The barrier between mankind and God was torn by the Atonement. Adam was free to return again to the Holy of Holies, the celestial kingdom, or the presence of God through the Atonement. The progression back to the tree of life was complete, through the Atonement.

Have you noticed by now that the profound lessons we have discussed about the Atonement are also profound lessons about the temple? When we learn of the temple, we really learn of the Atonement. This lesson, of the veil being torn when the Atonement was complete and the price of sin was paid, is no exception. With all of these lessons, it should be extremely clear that the purpose of the temple really is to put the Atonement into full effect in our lives. Elder Talmage taught us that "No jot, iota, or tittle of the temple rites is otherwise than uplifting and sanctifying. In every detail the endowment ceremony contributes to covenants of morality of life, consecration of person to high ideals, devotion to truth, patriotism to nation, and allegiance to God."[12] Quite simply, this is true because every jot, iota, and tittle (which means every last detail) of the temple experience points to Christ.

SUMMARY

- Moses and Aaron were the principal figures in the ancient temple or Tabernacle. Their roles in the plan of salvation directly point to the Son of God.
- The Aaronic Priesthood brings people to Christ and prepares them for the blessings of the Melchizedek Priesthood, which was originally called the Holy Priesthood, after the Order of the Son of God. The Aaronic Priesthood does not have the power to administer all of the ordinances necessary to return to the presence of God, but its purpose is to bring people to Christ. Christ

and the Melchizedek Priesthood have the power to bring people back to the Father.

- The Mosaic law also served to point people to Christ. This law did not have the power of salvation, but, like the Aaronic Priesthood, its purpose was to bring people to Christ. This emphasizes the role of Christ in bringing people back to the Father.

- The ancient temple was divided into three sections: the outer courtyard, the holy place, and the Holy of Holies. These divisions represent the telestial, terrestrial, and celestial kingdoms.

- Sacrifice and obedience are the first principles taught by the ancient temple. These principles prepare us for greater covenants and ordinances that can return us to the Holy of Holies.

- The ordinance of washing and anointing was performed in the ancient temple and is performed in the temple today. Like baptism and the sacrament, this ordinance represents another birth of water and the spirit that lead us back to salvation.

- The sacrament and prayer are also represented in the holy place, which is symbolic of the terrestrial kingdom.

- The Holy of Holies represents the tree of life or the celestial kingdom. The veil—the barrier that separates the holy place from the Holy of Holies—was and is torn by the Atonement of Christ.

Notes

1. Joseph Smith, *Teachings of the Prophet Joseph Smith*, 91.
2. The apocryphal Testament of Levi records a visit between the Lord and Levi in which the Lord instructs, "Levi, I have given thee the blessings of the priesthood until I come and sojourn in the midst of Israel." This explanation of Levi's priesthood follows the same pattern: The Aaronic or Levitical Priesthood was given in order to carry Israel through until the Lord's coming in the flesh. With the

restoration of the gospel, the Aaronic Priesthood is given in order to carry modern-day Israel through until the Lord's second coming (D&C 13). In all these instances, the Aaronic Priesthood leads directly to Jesus Christ, His Priesthood, and His reign on Earth.

3. Jacob Neusner, *Religion and Theology*, Vol. 3, 94–95.

4. Ibid.

5. Remember that this act of clothing fits one of the definitions of endowment, namely, "to clothe."

6. Joseph Fielding McConkie & Donald W. Parry, *A Guide to Scriptural Symbols*, 88.

7. *The Ninth Temple—A Light in the Desert*, compiled by Evan Tye Peterson, 420–21.

8. In the Church, we usually note that the sacrament serves to renew our baptismal covenants. However, no scripture directly limits the sacrament's purpose of renewal to baptismal covenants. The fact that the emblems of the sacrament are present in the ancient temple might suggest that the sacrament serves to renew our temple covenants as well as our baptismal covenants.

9. Brigham Young, *Discourses of Brigham Young*, 416.

10. According to *Strong's*, the Greek verb translated in Matthew 27:51 as "rent" is the same verb used in the account of the Savior's baptism in Mark 1:10, where it is translated as "opened." "And straightway coming up out of the water, he saw the heavens *opened*, and the Spirit like a dove descending upon him: And there came a voice from heaven, saying, Thou art my beloved Son, in whom I am well pleased." Apparently the verb presented a difficulty for the New Testament translators in Mark, as they couldn't figure how the heavens could be rent or divided. This further emphasizes the relationship between baptism and the temple. In both instances, the heavens were "rent" following a divine act. In the first case, the heavens were rent with the Savior's baptism. In the second case, the veil of the temple was rent with the

final payment of the debt for sin.

11. James E. Talmage, *The House of the Lord*, 84.

CHAPTER 6

WORTHINESS TO ENTER THE TEMPLE

The best preparation to enter the temple is the process of becoming worthy to enter the temple. Your worthiness to be in the temple will allow you to have the Holy Ghost to help you put the pieces of the puzzle together.

At the time of Christ, the Levites (the family group in charge of temple administration) set up night watches to make sure nobody entered the temple unworthily.

> At night guards were placed in twenty-four stations about the gates and courts. Of these, twenty-one were occupied by Levites alone; the other innermost three jointly by priests and Levites. Each guard consisted of ten men; so that in all two hundred and forty Levites and thirty priests were on duty every night. During the night the captain of the Temple made his rounds. On his approach the guards had to rise and salute him in a particular manner. Any guard found asleep when on duty was beaten, or his garments were set on fire—a punishment, as we know, actually awarded.[1]

As you might have guessed, the protections against someone entering the temple unworthily are a little bit different today. The Lord's system now is based on obtaining and presenting a recommend. This recommend is signed by the person entering the temple, that person's bishop (or a member of the bishopric if it is a renewed recommend), and stake president (or member of the stake presidency, again, if it is a renewed recommend). Including the member himself, all three of these people sign the recommend as a verification of the person's worthiness to enter the temple. The one entering the temple must be living in accordance with certain gospel laws and principles. We show the recommend to someone at the front desk of the temple, and we are allowed to enter.

What we need to understand is that this process of obtaining a temple recommend is a blessing. It is a process of testimony building, worthiness, and purification. This process is in fact the best temple preparation of all because it invites the Spirit, and there is no better assistant in identifying and fitting the puzzle pieces together than the Holy Ghost.

WHO SHALL ASCEND THE HILL OF THE LORD?

Who shall ascend into the hill of the Lord? or who shall stand in his holy place?

He that hath clean hands, and a pure heart; who hath not lifted up his soul unto vanity, nor sworn deceitfully.

He shall receive the blessing from the Lord, and righteousness from the God of his salvation (Psalms 24:3–5).

This scripture summarizes the qualifications to enter the Lord's house. We learned earlier that whenever we see a reference to a mountain (the Hebrew word in the text, *har*, means "mountain" but was translated as "hill" in this verse for some reason) in the scriptures, it's really a reference to a temple experience. The requirements to "ascend into the hill [mountain] of the Lord" and "stand in his holy place" are:

- Clean hands
- A pure heart
- A soul that is not vain (i.e., a humble soul)
- Lips that haven't sworn (i.e., a clean mouth)

These qualifications are principles. They are not specific questions in the temple recommend interview, but they form the basis for the specific questions in the interview. If we are living these basic principles, then we should have no problem giving the proper answers to the questions in the temple recommend interview. Therefore, before we get into some of the specific qualifications for obtaining a recommend, we will examine the principles that form the basis of the laws we need to live.

Clean Hands—Our hands represent our deeds, our actions. If they have been soiled, so to speak, by deeds and actions that keep us from entering the house of the Lord, it's time to wash them.

Notice that we are not required to present hands that have never been soiled; we only need to present hands that are clean. As we've all sinned, the real issue is whether we have repented or not. Even Joseph Smith, the man who has done more for the salvation of mankind than any other man except Jesus (D&C 135:3) found a great need to examine his heart and repent. "Search your hearts, and see if you are like God. I have searched mine, and feel to repent of all my sins."[2] The shame is not so much in *needing* to repent, but in *failing* to repent.

When I was a senior in high school, it was my privilege in writing for the school newspaper to interview a teacher who was retiring that year. He was a legend at the high school. In addition to being a wise and a wonderful teacher for many, many years, he had many sons who had gone through the high school and accomplished wonderful things. One of those sons was a starting quarterback in the NFL at the time. Another was a major league baseball player. This was a fabulous teacher and a fabulous man. My paragraph here doesn't begin to do him justice. When interviewing him, my friend and I asked him for some parting words of wisdom that he could leave for the institution and students he had blessed so greatly for so long.

His answer was timeless. "Pay the price," he said.

When it comes to repentance, I echo his words: Pay the price.

Whatever that price is, it is worth it and so much more. Washing our hands is a divine privilege, not a curse. Whatever the issue is that requires repentance to enter the temple, the blessing that awaits you is worth it a thousand times over. Whatever shade of scarlet we start with on our hands, it is a joy to wash them white (Isaiah 1:18).

A Pure Heart—Our heart often represents our deepest desires. Purifying our hearts is an ongoing process, and it tends to go hand in hand with cleansing our hands. It is possible to have clean hands without having a pure heart, but the process to obtain both clean hands and a pure heart is much the same. Like every other blessing we have mentioned, the key is in the Atonement of the Savior.

> And they had viewed themselves in their own carnal state, even less than the dust of the earth. And they all cried aloud with one voice, saying: O have mercy, and apply the atoning blood of Christ that we may receive *forgiveness of our sins,* and our *hearts may be purified;* for we believe in Jesus Christ, the Son of God, who created heaven and earth, and all things; who shall come down among the children of men (Mosiah 4:2; emphasis added).

A Soul That Is Not Vain—Humility is a prerequisite to entering the temple worthily. Your recommend interview will not use the word "humble," but humility remains the key to offering a broken heart and contrite spirit (3 Nephi 9:20). This is the sacrifice that the Lord asks of us. If we have this, we will be willing to offer any other sacrifice and keep any other commandment we may ever be asked to.

Taking these last two conditions together—a pure heart and a soul that is not vain—we have a heart and soul. This combination covers not just our deepest desires, but also our thoughts as well. Alma the Younger taught that we would be judged by our works, our thoughts, and our words (Alma 12:14). We have already discussed our works, and according to Alma and the Psalmist, the same purification process is needed for our thoughts as well.

Lips That Haven't Sworn Deceitfully—Our words are the last subject mentioned by Alma, and they are the last subject mentioned in Psalms 24 as well. Isaiah feared his own temple experience because he viewed himself as "a man of unclean lips" (Isaiah 6:5). To purge and clean his lips, an angel touched a live coal to them (Isaiah 6:7). The suggestion is not to burn your mouth before you enter the temple; rather, as with everything else we have discussed, the suggestion is to repent of any problem that may keep you from entering the temple.

These principles form the framework for the qualifications required to receive a temple recommend. If your thoughts, deeds, words, and heart are clean, the blessing is yours.

Opening Our Hands, Heart, Mind, and Lips to Heaven—Interestingly, there is a practice recorded in the scriptures that illustrates all these principles at the same time. Many scriptures describe people praying with their hands lifted toward heaven (Ezra 9:5; Psalms 141:2; 1 Timothy 2:8; D&C 88:135). In one of these scriptures, the prayer is offered by a person who is facing the temple (1 Kings 8:38, 54).

This posture of prayer with uplifted hands puts everything in full view of the Lord. These raised hands are the universal sign of surrender. In this case, the surrender is to the Lord. The hands, lips, heart, and mind are all exposed to the Lord. Nothing is hidden. Symbolically, all the elements of Psalms 24 are opened to the Lord for His inspection of the one offering the prayer.[3] In this way, the person offering the prayer is surrendering his will completely to the Lord. The Lord is free to observe whether the person has met the qualifications to ascend the hill of the Lord and stand in the holy place.

PREPARING TO RECEIVE A TEMPLE RECOMMEND

One important note on worthiness: Don't panic. You are not required to be perfect. You are only required to be worthy, and worthiness on this Earth is not the same as perfection. If you are truly keeping your baptismal covenants, then you will be fine with the temple recommend interview questions. If you are fine with the temple recommend interview questions, then you are worthy to enter the temple. The Church's temple preparation class addresses some specific commandments that we must be living in order to qualify for a recommend and be fine with this process.

Moral Cleanliness—The first of these commandments that we must be living is the law of chastity. Elder Talmage's summary of the endowment includes a promise to live this law.

On the subject of chastity, President Hinckley said, "We believe in chastity before marriage and total fidelity after marriage. That sums it up. That is the way to happiness in living. That is the way to satisfaction. It brings peace to the heart and peace to the home."[4]

Remember our observation in the vocabulary chapter about the word "profane." When something sacred is kept within the bounds set by the Lord, it remains sacred, uplifting, and beautiful. When that sacred thing is taken out of its proper place, it becomes egregious. This is a perfect illustration of the law of chastity. Keeping your desires and actions within the bounds of marriage preserves the sanctity of the powers of procreation.

Moral temptation is the adversary's three-hundred-mile-per-hour fastball. Don't even step up to the plate against this pitch! The best you can hope to do against this pitch is strike out. More likely, the adversary will throw this pitch right at your head, and I don't know anybody who can withstand a three-hundred-mile-per-hour fastball to the head, or any other part of the body. This adversary is not like any other foe you'll face or see in movies. You don't beat him by confronting him. You only beat this enemy by staying away from him altogether, and especially this particular pitch. He wrecks more lives with moral temptations than with any other pitch, perhaps even more than all others combined. If you are following the plain and simple guidelines set forth by President Hinckley, you are morally worthy to enter the temple.

Tithing—Elder Talmage's summary of the endowment tells us that, in the temple, we make covenants to dedicate our time and material blessings to the cause of truth. The law of tithing prepares us to make this covenant. "The simplest statement we know of is the statement of the Lord himself, namely, that the members of the Church should pay 'one-tenth of all their interest annually,' which is understood to mean income."[5] The adversary will be thrilled if he can mow people down with the law of chastity, but he will still be delighted to keep them from the temple any way he can. In my experience, he loves to attack the law of tithing to keep good, honest, and moral members of the Church away from the temple. Truth be told, obedience to this commandment opens not just the windows of heaven, but also the doors of the temple (Malachi 3:10).

To help understand the law of tithing, think for a minute how it helps prepare us to enter the temple. I have long believed that, if He wanted to, the Lord could easily tell His prophet to buy up some property in a remote corner of the world that would reveal the richest diamond, oil, or gold deposit on the planet. To date, He hasn't done that or anything like it. The Lord could finance His church any way he wants to, and He has chosen the law of tithing to do so. I believe the reason for this is simple and straightforward: We need to learn the principle of sacrifice for our own good.

Joseph Smith taught that, "A religion that does not require the sacrifice of all things never has power sufficient to produce the faith necessary unto life and salvation."[6] The goal of the temple is eternal life. That road requires the sacrifice of all things. Tithing is the starting point on the road to being able to offer all things unto the Lord. It exists for our good, not the Lord's.

The Word of Wisdom—No matter what you might think, this is a spiritual, not a physical commandment (D&C 29:31–34). Like tithing, the Word of Wisdom is also a kind of preparatory commandment. Many people are surprised to know that a form of the Word of Wisdom was given anciently, not just today. It was given as a requirement for the priests officiating in the ancient temple.

> And the Lord spake unto Aaron, saying,
> Do not drink wine nor strong drink, thou, nor thy sons with thee, when ye go into the tabernacle of the congregation, lest ye die: it shall be a statute for ever throughout your generations:
> And that ye may put difference between holy and unholy, and between unclean and clean;
> And that ye may teach the children of Israel all the statutes

which the Lord hath spoken unto them by the hand of Moses (Leviticus 10:8–11).

In the ancient temple, the version of the Word of Wisdom given to Aaron and his sons was the "difference between holy and unholy, and between unclean and clean."

This is a preparatory commandment because it opens the door to greater blessings. As we are promised:

> And all saints who remember to keep and do these sayings, *walking in obedience to the commandments,* shall receive health in their navel and marrow to their bones;
> And shall find wisdom and great treasures of knowledge, even hidden treasures;
> And shall run and not be weary, and shall walk and not faint.
> And I, the Lord, give unto them a promise, that the destroying angel shall pass by them, as the children of Israel, and not slay them. Amen (D&C 89:18–21; emphasis added).

The blessings that come from this commandment are not only the difference between holiness and unholiness, but they also open the door to wisdom, knowledge, and even hidden treasures. This commandment opens doors—including the temple doors—to so many other blessings.

The Sabbath Day—Like tithing, what is this commandment preparing us for? How much holiness can we truly expect if we offer the Lord only one day a week? Like tithing, this commandment prepares us to offer our whole souls to the Lord (Omni 1:26). We begin to offer our whole lives to the Lord literally one day at a time, and the Sabbath is specifically set aside for this purpose.

CONCLUSION

President Howard W. Hunter extended an open invitation to the Church that will never expire or grow old.

> I . . . invite the members of the Church to establish the temple of the Lord as the great symbol of their membership and the super-nal setting for their most sacred covenants. It would be the deepest

desire of my heart to have every member of the Church be temple worthy. I would hope that every adult member would be worthy of—and carry—a temple recommend.[7]

The process of obtaining a temple recommend is a great blessing and should be the goal of every Latter-day Saint. The blessings of the temple are the most choice and profound blessings that we can receive in mortality. This is why these blessings have been "kept hid from before the foundation of the world" (D&C 124:38). They are beyond the spiritual understanding and righteousness level of most of the world. Anciently, very few people were permitted to enter the tabernacle and the temple in Jerusalem.

There has never been a period in history when these blessings were as available as they are today. These blessings are not given to just anyone. They are available to *everyone who is worthy*. That worthiness is well within your reach.

SUMMARY

- At the time of Christ, up to 240 people guarded the temple to make sure that no one entered it unworthily. Today we use the process of a temple recommend to ensure worthiness to enter the temple.
- Clean hands, a pure heart, a humble mind, and a clean mouth are the principles of righteousness that encompass the temple recommend interview questions.
- Some of the laws that we must live in order to qualify for a temple recommend include the law of chastity, tithing, the Word of Wisdom, and keeping the Sabbath day holy. In many ways, these commandments serve to prepare us for the greater laws and covenants of the temple.
- President Hunter invited every member of the Church to make the temple the center of our worship and the symbol of our membership in the Church. He also invited all adult members to be worthy of a temple recommend and

to carry that recommend with them.

- The blessings of the temple have never been more available than they are today. They are available to everyone who is worthy.

Notes

1. Alfred Edersheim, *The Temple—Its Ministry and Services as They Were at the Time of Christ*, 147–48.

2. *History of the Church*, 4:588, from a discourse given by Joseph Smith on April 10, 1842, reported by Wilford Woodruff.

3. Donald W. Parry, "Temple Worship and a Possible Reference to a Prayer Circle in Psalm 24."

4. Gordon B. Hinckley, "This Thing Was Not Done in a Corner," *Ensign*, Nov. 1996.

5. First Presidency Letter, March 19, 1970.

6. Joseph Smith, *Lectures on Faith*, 69.

7. Howard W. Hunter, *Ensign*, July 1994.

Chapter 7

The Blessings of the Temple

The Road to the Temple

I vividly remember one evening from my high school years. I ran into a high school track teammate at the store, and we began talking about things in general. To be honest, I was pretty flattered that she was even talking to me. She was the homecoming queen, the top student in her class, a model, and already a world-class athlete. I was, well, none of the above.

One of us mentioned the three-hundred-meter intermediate hurdles, an event that we both ran. She very humbly stated that she "really needed to work" on her time in that event. (I read in the paper later that week that her best time in the event was the third fastest recorded in the entire country that year. And I don't even think it was her best event. She was being very humble and gracious indeed.)

The conversation then turned, and she asked if I would be running at an invitational track meet later that week. She was LDS, so I didn't hesitate to tell her that I wouldn't be there because it was my ward's turn to go to the temple and do baptisms for the dead. All these years later, I will never forget her reply. "Oh, that's probably more important." Yes, I agreed with her. And today I would agree even more heartily.

The years since then have been a most interesting contrast between our two paths. She went on to grace the cover of magazines and to be a world-renowned athlete. She has proudly represented the United States in multiple Olympic Games. This is a wonderful goal for any young athlete to follow. Think about it—representing your country in the Olympics is probably a one in a million chance. But, to my knowledge, she never made it to the temple, and she hasn't been active in the Church in years.

I've never been and never will be on the cover of any magazine. Likewise, if I ever make it to the Olympics, it will only be as a spectator. But I have been to the House of the Lord, and I don't have to wait every four years to return there.

The directions she and I were each taking that night have summed up life since then. Her road took her to the Olympics. My road took me to the temple. I wouldn't trade places with her in a million years.

Considering all of the people who have lived on the Earth, those who enter the temple during their lives are probably about as common as those who make it to the Olympics. However, it doesn't have to be that way. Most people who dream of making an Olympic team will never make it because they simply don't have the talent. They just don't have the God-given ability in them to be among the super-elite athletes on the Earth.

On the other hand, there is no such talent restriction on making it to the temple. *Anyone* who truly dreams of partaking of the Lord's choicest blessings can receive those blessings through the temple. *Anyone* who pursues the temple with anywhere near the dedication shown by an elite athlete training for the Olympics can and will make it to the temple.

My old high school teammate will undoubtedly treasure her Olympic memories forever. I know I would. Great events are that way: You spend a very short time living the moment and a lifetime remembering it.

But the temple is quite different. You spend a relatively short time living the moment, and you spend literally an eternity receiving the blessings from it. That is why I wouldn't trade places with my friend in a million years. No great memory or even any lifetime of memories is worth trading for the blessings of the temple and the eternity that can follow. The road to the temple is the only road to the kind of eternity that our Father in Heaven wants to give us.

The Blessings of the Temple

We do a pretty good job of teaching the blessings and importance of the temple in the Church. We are taught early on in Primary that we should live our lives preparing to go to the temple some day. There are a number of wonderful books on the temple whose main message is of the blessings of the temple. We have spent most of this book teaching about the blessing of man's return to being like God and eventually being with God, and rightly so. This blessing is so great that it subsumes every other eternal blessing. However, there are other blessings that accompany this great blessing, and receiving and understanding them makes life so very much better.

Among these blessings are:

- The blessing of cleanliness
- The blessing of protection
- The blessing of eternal families
- The blessing of being born in the covenant

This is by no means an exhaustive list of blessings from the temple. The list of such blessings is literally endless. We will explore a few of these blessings in hopes of encouraging temple attendance and study that are necessary to receive even more blessings that await us in the House of the Lord.

The Blessing of Cleanliness

I earlier stated that my first real impression after receiving my endowment was not one of spiritual understanding, but of cleanliness. I felt clean—so clean that my lack of understanding about the endowment didn't really bother me. Sure, I was determined to learn what the Lord was trying to teach me, but I very much enjoyed basking in the Spirit and the cleanliness I felt.

This is the same blessing of cleanliness from the temple that President Joseph F. Smith taught about.

> I dreamed [one night] that I was on a journey, and I was impressed that I ought to hurry—hurry with all my might, for fear I might be too late. I rushed on my way as fast as I possibly could, and I was only conscious of having just a little bundle, a handkerchief with a small bundle wrapped in it. I did not realize just what it was, when I was hurrying as fast as I could; but finally I came to a wonderful mansion. . . . I thought I knew that was my destination. As I passed toward it, as fast as I could, I saw a notice, 'Bath.' I turned aside quickly and went into the bath and washed myself clean. I opened up this little bundle that I had, and there was a pair of white, clean garments, a thing I had not seen for a long time, because the people I was with did not think very much of making things exceedingly clean. But my garments were clean, and I put them on. Then I rushed to what appeared to be a great opening, or door. I knocked and the door opened, and the man who stood there was the Prophet Joseph Smith. He looked at me a little reprovingly, and the first words he said: "Joseph, you are late." Yet I took confidence and replied:
>
> "Yes, but I am clean—I am clean!"
>
> He clasped my hand and drew me in, then closed the great door. I felt his hand just as tangible as I ever felt the hand of man. I knew him, and when I entered I saw my father, and Brigham [Young] and Heber [C. Kimball], and Willard [Richards], and other good men that I had known, standing in a row. It looked as if it were across this valley, and it seemed to be filled with a vast multitude of people, but on the stage were all the people that I had known. My mother was there, and she sat with a child in her lap; and I could name over as many as I remember of their names, who sat there, who seemed to be among the chosen, among the exalted. . . .
>
> [When I had this dream] I was alone on a mat, away up in the mountains of Hawaii—no one was with me. But in this vision I pressed my hand up against the Prophet, and I saw a smile cross his countenance. . . .
>
> When I awoke that morning I was a man, although only a boy.

There was not anything in the world that I feared [after that]. I could meet any man or woman or child and look them in the face, feeling in my soul that I was a man every whit. That vision, that manifestation and witness that I enjoyed at that time has made me what I am, if I am anything that is good, or clean, or upright before the Lord, if there is anything good in me. That has helped me out in every trial and through every difficulty.[1]

This is the blessing of cleanliness that comes from being washed and clothed in the Lord's house.

THE BLESSING OF PROTECTION

A few days after I received my endowment, I went to a nearby lake with several of my friends who were also set to leave on their missions soon. Water skiing is not an appropriate activity to wear the temple garments, so this meant that I would need to leave my garments for a few hours while we went to the lake. Well, we had fun that day, but I felt somewhat empty and awkward without my garments. I honestly could not wait to get back home and get properly dressed again. In just a few short days, I had grown to love the feeling of cleanliness and spiritual wholeness from the reminders of my new covenants so much that I could not bear to be without them, even for just a few hours.

My own protection is one thing, but the protection of those I love is a far more serious issue. As parents of five beautiful daughters, my wife and I are always seeking to protect them in one way or another. We don't let a day go by without praying for them. We have been entrusted with them to get them back to their eternal home safely and worthily. That is no small responsibility, and it is one that we certainly need divine help to fulfill.

On that note, I point you to a story from Michael Wilcox about some family blessings of protection from the temple that were promised to him through the Spirit.

When I moved to Utah ten years ago, my children were entering their teenage years. Having taught teenagers in seminary, I knew how critical the next years would be, for during these years we win or lose so many battles for the souls of men. The more I thought about the world my children were growing up in and the pressures and opposition arrayed against them, the more anxious I felt.

I went to the temple one afternoon to seek guidance about my children. The calm, loving spirit of the temple seemed to magnify my natural love for my family, and I found myself offering a deeply sincere prayer filled with desire for my children. I told the Lord I was willing to offer any sacrifice if he would protect my children from Satan's power and bless them with his Spirit until they could come to his house and receive their own endowment. I do not think I offered a unique prayer. It is the uttered and unuttered prayer of every true Latter-day Saint parent, and I think most parents would give the Lord the sacrifice he required.

As I sat in the temple, an answer was given in which the required sacrifice was revealed to me. I thought the Lord would demand some great thing for the blessing I was asking, and had it been some great thing, I believe I would have been willing to fulfill it. Often we are more willing to do the great things than the small, everyday acts of obedience and sacrifice that comprise living the gospel.

However, the Spirit simply whispered: "This is the sacrifice I ask of you. Be in this house *frequently, constantly,* and *consistently,* and the promised protection you seek, which this house has the power to bestow, will be extended to those you love." For that blessing alone I would be in the temple as often as I could.[2]

I can think of no greater insurance policy for our loved ones than to be in the House of the Lord frequently, constantly, and consistently, as Brother Wilcox shares.

THE BLESSING OF ETERNAL FAMILIES

There's a world of meaning in the simple phrase, "families can be together forever."

One evening my teenage niece called me, very concerned over something she had been told about the concept of an eternal family. Her father had left the Church years ago and had not been faithful to his covenants. She was quite mistakenly told that she would not be sealed to any of her family in the eternities because of her father's choices. Now, this is a young woman who lives with an eye toward the eternities and is very intent on keeping all of her covenants. With this in mind, I assured her that there was no such thing as a righteous orphan in the eternities. Somehow, the chain of righteous family members will extend all the way back to Adam. There is a place for my wonderful niece, and anyone else who makes and keeps the covenants of the temple, in this chain. I am sure that many people who have lost their place in the chain can have it restored if they will pay the price. Regardless, someone else's weak or missing link will not leave the righteous out of the chain.

A few years back, I received just a hint of what it means to have an eternal family and to be a part of this eternal chain. I count it as perhaps the most special moment of life. My oldest niece was getting married, and my oldest nephew was leaving on his mission. Both were receiving their endowment on the same day in the same temple.

Three generations were gathered together in the temple that day. Extended family members and loved ones were also filling the temple. What impressed me so deeply was that every link in our part of the chain was present and accounted for. Most of us had traveled several hundred miles to be there, but we *were* there, and we were there worthily. As we were all gathered in white in the temple, I saw just a hint of what an eternal family is like. Again, it was only a hint, but it was enough to move me deeply and help me look forward to the day when my own children could join us.

The day my wife and I were sealed was also accompanied by an outpouring of the Spirit that filled my eyes with tears. That was a day of promise, a day of looking forward to everything that was yet to come, if we were worthy. But as more people gathered and another generation entered the temple that special day many years later, my eyes were opened further. It was still a day of promise and optimism for the future, but it was also a day of promises realized, as I saw one more generation of my family and one more generation of links in the chain come to the temple in righteousness. I can only imagine how it will be when my wife and I can bring our own daughters to the temple worthily. One day we hope to do the same for our grandchildren. These future days will be days of promise that give only a glimpse of the true eternal family that awaits us in the eternities through the temple and through covenants made and kept.

Now I don't know exactly how this chain of eternal families will be forged in the eternities or how weak or missing links will be accounted for. Likewise, I don't know of any specific or definitive statement by any Church leaders about how this chain will be put together. Even the great prophet Brigham Young was not able to express in words how the eternal family would be forged. He spoke of a vision in which Joseph Smith appeared to him in an effort to help explain how eternal families would fit together on the other side of the veil. Joseph told Brigham, "Our Father in Heaven organized the human family, but they are all disorganized and in great confusion." Brigham continued, "Joseph then showed me the pattern, how they were in the beginning. This I cannot describe, but I saw it, and saw where the Priesthood had been taken from the Earth and how it must be joined together, so that there would be a perfect chain from Father Adam to his latest posterity."[3]

If Brigham Young, of all people, could not describe in words how the eternal family will fit together, then I certainly couldn't describe it either. What I do know, is that the promised blessing will be ours if we are worthy.

In the first case I mentioned, about my teenage niece, I only know that she will not be an eternal orphan if she is righteous. I don't know all the specifics of how Heavenly Father will construct her eternal family in her earthly father's chosen absence from the blessings of the temple. I only know that Heavenly Father's promise is sure. Where covenants are made and kept, the blessing will come. No maker and keeper of temple covenants will be alone in the eternities. In fact, when the Savior promised His disciples that he would not leave them "comfortless," He really told them that He would not leave them "orphans."[4] While we don't understand the meaning of all things or the precise way that the blessing will be given, we can rest assured that our Father loves His children (1 Nephi 11:17). There is literally an eternity to sort out and unfold these blessings for the worthy.

The Blessing of Being Born in the Covenant

Children born to parents who have been sealed in the temple are literally "born in the covenant." This means they are born with the blessings of being sealed to their family, and those blessings are theirs to lose. They are born as links of a chain of righteous family members, leading all the way back to Adam. As long as they don't break the chain, the blessings are theirs beyond the grave and for eternity.

Children born into the covenant are also entitled to a special level of spiritual help in this life. "They may receive a greater guidance, a greater protection, a greater inspiration from the Spirit of the Lord."[5] This greater blessing will keep them closer to the fold both spiritually and in terms of the eternal chain of family.

The best explanation of this blessing I have found comes from Elder Russell M. Nelson.

> Several years ago my son and his wife had born to them a beautiful child, but she had severe health challenges. She stayed here on earth with us only four months. . . . I went to the hospital and held her hand and talked with her as only a grandfather could. I received the peaceful assurance that Sarah [the granddaughter] always would be ours and wouldn't be here longer. I felt she was saying to me, 'It's all right, Grandpa.' I suggested to my son and his wife that we go to their home. We knelt in prayer. Because of the temple, and because my son and his wife had been sealed in the temple and Sarah was born under the covenant, we knew we could let her go and she would still be ours forever.[6]

That, my friends, is what it means to be born in the covenant.

SUMMARY

In closing, let me defer to Ezra Taft Benson, a prophet of God who not only summarized the blessings of the temple, but reiterated them as promises.

> Now let me say something else to all who can worthily go to the House of the Lord. When you attend the temple and perform the ordinances that pertain to the House of the Lord, certain blessings will come to you:
>
> - You will receive the spirit of Elijah, which will turn your hearts to your spouse, to your children, and to your forebears.
> - You will love your family with a deeper love than you have loved before.
> - Your hearts will be turned to your fathers and theirs to you.
> - You will be endowed with power from on high as the Lord has promised.
> - You will receive the key of the knowledge of God (See D&C 84:19). You will learn how you can be like Him. Even the power of godliness will be manifest to you (See D&C 84:20).
> - You will be doing a great service to those who have passed to the other side of the veil in order that they might be "judged according to men in the flesh, but live according to God in the spirit" (D&C 138:34).
>
> Such are the blessings of the temple and the blessings of frequently attending the temple.
>
> So I say: God bless Israel! God bless those of our forebears who constructed the holy temples. God bless us to teach our children and our grandchildren what great blessings await them by going to the temple. God bless us to receive all the blessings revealed by Elijah the prophet so that our callings and election will be made sure.
>
> I testify with all my soul to the truth of this message and pray that the God of Abraham, Isaac, and Jacob will bless modern Israel with the compelling desire to seek all the blessings of the fathers in the House of our Heavenly Father.[7]

Notes

1. Joseph F. Smith, *Gospel Doctrine*, 542–43.
2. S. Michael Wilcox, *House of Glory*, 47–48.

3. *Manuscript History of Brigham Young, 1846–1847,* Elden J. Watson, ed., 528–30.
4. Footnote, John 14:18. See also *Strong's Exhaustive Concordance of the Bible,* which notes that the Greek word used in the verse is *orphanos,* which we recognize as the root of the English word "orphans."
5. Joseph Fielding Smith, *Doctrines of Salvation, Vol 2,* 90.
6. Russell M. Nelson, *Church News,* October 31, 1992.
7. Ezra Taft Benson, "What I Hope You Will Teach Your Children about the Temple," *Ensign,* Aug. 1985.

CHAPTER 8

THE ORDINANCES AND COVENANTS OF THE TEMPLE

In the temple, we receive the ordinances that will enable us to return to the presence of God. Ordinances are sacred and symbolic acts that are outward expressions of inner commitments in the gospel. Ordinances in the gospel are accompanied by covenants. "The gospel is so arranged that principles and ordinances are received by covenant placing the recipient under strong obligation and responsibility to honor the commitment."[1] Therefore, when we receive the temple ordinances that we need in order to return to the presence of God and be like God, we make promises (covenants) to do certain things and to abstain from doing certain things. In return, the Lord promises us special and specific blessings as we make and keep these covenants.

Elder Talmage taught us what the basic covenants and ordinances of the temple are.

> The ordinances of the endowment embody certain obligations on the part of the individual, such as covenant and promise to observe the law of strict virtue and chastity; to be charitable, benevolent, tolerant and pure; to devote both talent and material means to the spread of truth and the uplifting of the race; to maintain devotion to the cause of truth; and to seek in every way to contribute to the great preparation that the earth may be made ready to receive her King,—the Lord Jesus Christ. With the taking of each covenant and

ach obligation a promised blessing is pronounced,
he faithful observance of the conditions.[2]

lerstand and apply these covenants to our lives
into the puzzle, we first need to understand
so important, how they are related with ordi-
ney both work.

Covenants Define How We Live

As I have studied the temple more deeply, I have come to define life itself in terms of covenants. I have learned to break down how well we serve in our callings, in parenthood, in service opportunities, and in every other aspect of our lives as a product of covenants kept or not kept. The more I study and observe, the more convinced I am that life as a follower of Christ really does boil down to making and keeping covenants.

Our lives are meant to be lived in keeping covenants. The covenants of the temple are meant to shape and govern every aspect of our lives. They are meant to conform us to the image of our Father in Heaven (JST Romans 8:29). They are meant to make us worthy to return to our heavenly home. Just as it is safe to conclude that the temple exists to put the Atonement into full practice, it is not an overstatement to conclude that a person's eternal life is defined by making and keeping sacred covenants. With the saving ordinances that accompany them, covenants hold the power to unlock the Atonement.

The Relationship between Covenants and Ordinances

Covenants are almost always mentioned with ordinances. A person may make personal covenants with the Lord that may not have accompanying ordinances. However, I cannot think of any gospel ordinances that do not have accompanying covenants.[3] The saving ordinances in particular, such as baptism and the temple ordinances, are meant to be a formal or symbolic lesson of the covenants that accompany them. These ordinances teach us both the importance of the covenant we are making *and* the blessings that come from keeping the covenant. They are meant to act as a symbol or a type of ratification ceremony to ourselves and the Lord that we have made the covenant and that we will keep the covenant.

Baptism is a perfect example of this relationship between saving ordinances and the covenants that accompany them. The covenant of baptism is a promise to take upon ourselves the name of Christ and stand as His witnesses always (Mosiah 18:10; D&C 20:37). We promise to give our lives in service so that our lives may be received by the Father. This is what we promise.

The ordinance involves washing with water and going completely under the water (3 Nephi 11:23–26). These actions symbolize the death of the natural man and a new birth of the follower of Christ (Romans 6:3–10). This is what we do in order to symbolize or ratify that promise before the Lord and the necessary witnesses.

The baptismal covenant involves taking a new name—the name of Christ—so sacred that we would never want to tarnish it or bring disrespect to it (Mosiah 5:8). We receive a name at birth, so this is a rebirth with a new name. Because of the name we take upon ourselves, we are now followers of Christ and members of His church. We are clean (D&C 39:10).

The covenant embodies and teaches this lesson in a dramatic way that is designed to penetrate our minds and hearts. We are buried in the water and then emerge as a reborn person. We are new and very, very clean. The ordinance reflects and symbolizes the covenant. The ordinance and covenant are separate, yet they are inseparably connected.

The saving ordinances of the temple are also highly symbolic. Just like baptism, they embody and reflect the covenants that accompany them. They reflect and mark the path of our progress through mortality back to the tree of life.

One of the most important lessons in the scriptures about

ordinances of the Priesthood teaches us that, "in the ordinances thereof, the power of godliness is manifest. And without the ordinances thereof, and the authority of the priesthood, the power of godliness is not manifest unto men in the flesh; For without this, no man can see the face of God, even the Father, and live" (D&C 84:20–22). This scripture teaches that we must have these ordinances in order to return to the tree of life or the presence of God. Since there are no saving ordinances without covenants, we can insert the word "covenants" right next to "ordinances."

But these scriptures teach more than just the necessity of ordinances and covenants. There is something very important about the statement that "in the ordinances thereof the power of godliness is manifest" (D&C 84:20). On the one hand, this scripture emphasizes that ordinances are essential, which, again, we already know. On the other hand, the scripture also suggests that there are lessons about godliness within the physical act of the ordinances themselves, just as with baptism. Therefore, the ordinances of the temple don't just lead to godliness; they symbolize and teach about godliness and the covenants that lead to godliness.

How Covenants Work: "Draw Near unto Me and I Will Draw Near unto You"

The simplest way I know of to describe how covenants work, is to say that we do our part, and the Lord does His. Between these two actions, man is brought together with God. This principle is illustrated by the words of the Lord Himself. "Draw near unto me, and I will draw near unto you; seek me diligently and ye shall find me; ask, and ye shall receive; knock, and it shall be opened unto you" (D&C 88:63). In each of these instances, we are the first participants. We draw near, we ask, we seek, and we knock.

Likewise, in each of these instances, the Lord is the second participant who bestows the blessing. After we draw near to Him, He draws near to us. After we seek, He reveals. After we ask, He gives. After we knock, He opens.[4]

Making and keeping covenants is what we do to draw near unto the Lord, to seek Him, to ask of Him and to knock on His door. As we do this, the Lord will draw near unto us, reveal Himself to us, give unto us, and open His door unto us. We do our part, and He does His. The end result is that we are brought in harmony with the Lord.

This is actually the concept symbolized by the Star of David. Many people are surprised to see this symbol, commonly associated with Judaism, on an LDS temple, but its meaning applies to all the House of Israel, not just to the tribe of Judah. It is comprised of two triangles that are overlapped or merged. One triangle points downward, representing God moving toward us. The second triangle points up, representing our movement toward God. When each side moves or does its part, so to speak, the triangles meet and overlap, and the Star of David is formed. We meet God, both symbolically and literally, through the temple. Through temple covenants, mankind becomes like God, Adam becomes Michael.

JACOB'S LADDER

This concept of covenant is beautifully illustrated by the prophet Jacob's vision, in which he found himself at the base of a ladder that reached from Earth all the way to heaven, where the Lord stood above it. He saw angels *ascending* and *descending* a ladder that reached from the Earth to heaven (Genesis 28:10–22). The movement in both directions reflects our movement toward God and His movement toward us. Sometimes He is reaching or sending angels down to help us, and other times He may be pulling us upwards. Again, this is how covenants work. We draw near unto the Lord, and the Lord draws near unto us. We seek, and He reveals Himself.

I have often wondered what the rungs on Jacob's ladder would be. What are the specific steps we need to take to climb this ladder? According to President Marion G. Romney, those rungs are none other than the covenants of the temple.

> Jacob realized that the covenants he made with the Lord were the rungs on the ladder that he himself would have to climb in order to obtain the promised blessings—blessings that would entitle him to enter heaven and associate with the Lord.
>
> Because he had met the Lord and entered into covenants with him there, Jacob considered the site so sacred that he named the place Bethel, a contraction of Beth-Elohim, which means literally "the House of the Lord." He said of it: ". . . this is none other but the house of God, and this is the gate of heaven" (Genesis 28:17).
>
> Jacob not only passed through the gate of heaven, but by living up to every covenant he also went all the way in. Of him and his forebears Abraham and Isaac, the Lord has said: ". . . because they did none other things than that which they were commanded, they have entered into their exaltation, according to the promises, and sit upon thrones, and are not angels but are gods (D&C 132:37).

Temples are to us what Bethel was to Jacob. Even more, they are also the gates to heaven for all of our unendowed kindred dead. We should all do our duty in bringing our loved ones through them.[5]

We climb to heaven by making and keeping sacred covenants. We progress through the world back to the tree of life by making and keeping these same covenants.

PRINCIPLES—THE SUPPORT FOR THE RUNGS ON THE LADDER

The rungs on a ladder are obviously very important, but so are the vertical supports that run along the sides of the rungs and keep them in place. If we think of the rungs on the ladder as ordinances and covenants, then we can think of the vertical parts of the ladder, supporting the rungs, as principles.

By principles, I mean the basis, lesson, or purpose for commandments and ordinances. For example, the commandment of tithing is based on the principles of sacrifice and faith. The commandment of the law of chastity is based on the principles of virtue and devotion. The ordinance of the sacrament is based on the principles of repentance and remembrance.

When we understand the principles of the gospel, we are better equipped to keep the commandments and covenants that are based on them. Since Adam and Eve's experience in the Garden of Eden, the Lord has always followed this pattern of teaching principles first and foremost. "Therefore God gave unto them commandments, *after* having made known unto them the plan of redemption, that they should not do evil" (Alma 12:32; emphasis added). In other words, before God gave Adam and Eve specific commandments, He taught them why they needed to obey those commandments and how their obedience would help bring them back to His presence. Like Adam and Eve, we understand and are better prepared to keep commandments if we understand the principles that support them.

This concept of principles supporting commandments is exactly what the Savior was referring to when he spoke: "Woe unto you, scribes and Pharisees, hypocrites! for ye pay tithe of mint and anise and cummin, and have omitted the weightier matters of the law, judgment, mercy and faith: these ought ye to have done, and not to leave the other undone" (Matthew 23:23). Focusing on rules or certain commandments at the expense of the principles or "weightier matters of the law" (such as mercy and faith) ultimately leads to a confusing of spiritual priorities. We begin to keep commandments for the wrong reasons and start going through the motions instead of being anxiously engaged in righteous causes. For example, we may keep the commandment of paying tithing, yet we often ignore or refuse other opportunities to serve and sacrifice, thereby betraying the principle that supports the commandment. At the same time, we may attend meetings, and yet somehow fail to worship. From that point, unrighteousness easily follows, just as it did with the scribes and Pharisees.

On the other hand, when we understand the principle behind the commandment, we are more likely to keep the commandment and be true to the principle behind it in our everyday lives. This is the everyday application of the temple and its covenants and ordinances.

Remember the lessons from the ancient temple. The most prominent lessons we learned from those symbols were principles such as sacrifice, obedience, the sacrament, and prayer. As you assemble the pieces of the puzzle in your modern temple experiences, look for the principles, not just the covenants and ordinances. To put it another way, look for the principles expressed *in* the covenants and ordinances. Understanding these principles and being true to them helps us treasure and keep the covenants we make in the temple and live our whole lives in accordance with those covenants.

THE COVENANTS OF THE TEMPLE

The specific covenants of the temple mentioned by Elder Talmage include:

- Virtue and chastity
- Charity, benevolence, tolerance and purity
- Devotion of talent and material means to the spread of truth and the building of the Kingdom of God to prepare the Earth for the King.[6]

These are familiar covenants because they are the same commandments we need to keep in order to obtain a temple recommend.

The covenant to devote our talents and material means to the Lord's kingdom is taught in the Doctrine and Covenants. In Section 104, the Lord outlines the United Order, which was a framework to allow the saints in Kirtland to live this commandment to its fullest extent. Note the specific directions on how the saints were to implement this principle and commandment.

"And they shall be organized in their own names, and in their own name; and they shall do their business in their own name, and in their own names; And you shall do your own business in your own name, and in your own names" (D&C 104:49–50). The saints were given this commandment individually (i.e., in their "own names") and collectively (i.e., in their "own name"). In this case, commandments and covenants of sacrifice were given individually and collectively. The saints were then and are still meant to unite and receive these commandments and covenants as a group as well as individually. Only when the saints are united can they really bring about the Zion that the Lord wants and that is required to exalt us (D&C 105:5).

As you put together the puzzle pieces that are the respective ordinances and covenants of the temple, remember that the power of godliness is manifest in these ordinances (D&C 84:20). Look for that power of godliness in those ordinances. Look for the ways that chastity, virtue, and devotion draw us nearer to God and make us more like Him individually and collectively.

THE HOLY SPIRIT OF PROMISE

I once heard a very learned man teach that the ordinance of temple marriage automatically seals a family for eternity. The key word there is "automatically," a basic synonym for "unconditionally." This is a severe misconception. The blessings promised to us in the temple are not unconditional; they are conditioned on our faithfulness. The act of receiving temple ordinances does not turn commandments into options. We must keep our promises and keep the commandments all the way through mortality. It's not enough just to make promises in the temple. We need to keep those promises in order to obtain the blessings.

This is where the Holy Spirit of Promise is important to understand. The Holy Spirit of Promise is a function of the Holy Ghost that ratifies, approves, or seals an ordinance (D&C 132:7, 19). The Holy Spirit of Promise's seal of approval on an ordinance is the difference between an eternal blessing being promised and being realized. It is the difference between becoming and being.

What does it take for the Holy Spirit of Promise to ratify an ordinance? Keeping the covenants that accompany the ordinance all our days. Faithfulness, pure and simple. When we receive the ordinances of the temple, the blessings of those ordinances become ours to lose. We can and will lose them if we don't keep the covenants that ensure them. President Harold B. Lee, speaking on this subject, explained that we may receive "the promise of power and authority, but it will not be ours—worlds without end—unless we keep our part of the covenant."[7]

Making covenants alone will not get us to the top of Jacob's ladder. We must spend our lives climbing that ladder by keeping the covenants we make. If we do not honor the covenants we have made, then the Holy Spirit of Promise cannot ratify those covenants. Disregarding sacred covenants puts us in danger of falling off of Jacob's ladder, and that can be a very long and painful fall.

To be clear—young men, your beautiful bride is only yours for eternity if you spend the rest of your days becoming and being worthy of her and treating her like a queen. She is only yours for eternity if you do not break the chain that extends from her to you to the Lord.

To all temple goers—when you have proven your worthiness and have sufficiently kept the covenants, then the Holy Spirit of Promise will remove the conditions from your eternity, and the blessings will be yours to keep. It will then be a matter of *being* like God, rather than working to *become* like God.

SUMMARY

- The ordinances and covenants of the temple are essential to our exaltation.
- Covenants and ordinances go hand in hand. Ordinances are usually outward expressions of the covenants they

accompany. Think of ordinances as ratification ceremonies or symbols of covenants.

- Our lives are defined by the covenants we make and keep. Covenants are agreements that draw us closer to God when we do our part and the Lord does His. We draw near unto Him, and He draws near unto us.

- According to Elder Talmage, the specific covenants of the temple include chastity, charity, benevolence, and sacrifice, even to the point of giving all our talent and material means to the Lord's cause on the Earth.

- These covenants and ordinances of the temple are the rungs on the ladder that Jacob saw in a vision, leading from Earth to heaven.

- If covenants and ordinances are the rungs on this ladder, then principles are the supports that hold the rungs together and keep them in place.

- The tokens and signs mentioned by President Young in his description of the endowment are part of the covenants and ordinances we make in the temple. They symbolize and give proof of our covenants.

- The Holy Spirit of Promise is a function of the Holy Ghost that ratifies ordinances. It is not enough just to receive temple ordinances; we must keep the covenants we make. Think of the Holy Spirit of Promise as making the difference between *becoming* clean and *being* clean.

Notes

1. LDS Bible Dictionary.
2. James E. Talmage, *The House of the Lord*, 84.
3. One possible exception may be a baby blessing. However, a baby blessing may be accurately called a mortal ordinance that accompanies a pre-mortal covenant. A child being born into this world (especially into the Church) must have made covenants in the pre-mortal life that brought the child into such blessings in this world (See Alma 13; Abraham 3). Based on this example, it may be appropriate

to say that some ordinances are received as a result of covenants made earlier.

4. See also D&C 109, which is the dedicatory prayer for the Kirtland temple. In verse eight, we are commanded to organize, establish, and so forth. In verses 14, 15, and 24, the same verbs appear, except this time it is the Lord who is organizing and establishing us. We seek the blessing and act accordingly, and the Lord bestows the blessing.

5. Marion G. Romney, "Temples–The Gates to Heaven," *Ensign*, Mar. 1971.

6. Talmage, *The House of the Lord*, 84.

7. Harold B. Lee, *Stand Ye in Holy Places*, 52.

CHAPTER 9

LEARNING FROM THE LORD THROUGH SYMBOLS

Virtually every facet of the temple experience contains symbolic lessons that can easily go unappreciated or even ignored by the casual observer. This method of symbolism is important to recognize up front. To learn the lessons from the symbols of the temple, we must be guided by the Spirit and understand what the Lord is trying to teach us through symbolism.

The Savior also taught in the New Testament by using symbolism. When the disciples asked the Lord why He taught in parables, a great form of symbolism, He responded:

> Because it is given unto you to know the mysteries of the kingdom of heaven, but to them it is not given.
>
> For whosoever hath, to him shall be given, and he shall have more abundance: but whosoever hath not, from him shall be taken away even that he hath.
>
> Therefore speak I to them in parables: because they seeing see not; and hearing they hear not, neither do they understand.
>
> And in them is fulfilled the prophecy of Esaias, which saith, By hearing ye shall hear, and shall not understand; and seeing ye shall see, and shall not perceive:
>
> For this people's heart is waxed gross, and their ears are dull of hearing, and their eyes they have closed; lest at any time they should see with their eyes, and hear with their ears, and should understand

with their heart, and should be converted, and I should heal them.

But blessed are your eyes, for they see: and your ears, for they hear (Matthew 13:11–16).

This lesson from the Lord Himself teaches us that symbolism has the unique ability both to conceal sacred truths from the unprepared and to reward those who are truly seeking to learn deep and meaningful lessons. The truths taught by symbolism will be kept from those who do not see or hear in a spiritual sense. When the unprepared soften their hearts and open their ears and eyes, they will understand what the Lord is teaching.

Nowhere is this more evident than in the temple. The truths of the temple have been "hid from before the world was" (D&C 124:38). By couching the great spiritual truths of the temple in symbolism, the spiritually prepared will learn the lessons one at a time, as they are ready. These same lessons will remain hidden in symbolism from those who are spiritually unprepared to receive them.

The impact of teaching with symbols is both a joy and a frustration to many people. It's a joy to learn great spiritual truths through symbolism because it has the power to make words more than just words. It deeply impresses truths on our minds and in our hearts.

At the same time, it can be a great frustration because it's so foreign. We just don't talk too much about symbolism in the Church. In most wards, it's safe to say that Sunday school lessons or sacrament meeting talks on symbolism are few and far between, if they are given at all. Because of our lack of familiarity with symbolism, we tend not to appreciate the lessons the Lord is trying to teach us and may even become frustrated by the symbolism. Unfortunately, it's human nature not to appreciate what we don't understand.

On this subject, Elder John A. Widtsoe taught:

> Some have gone through the temple looking at the outward form and not the inner meaning of things. The form of the endowment is of an earthly nature, but it symbolizes great spiritual truths. All that we do on this earth is earthly, but all is symbolic of great

spiritual truths. To build this temple, earth had to be dug; wood had to be cut; stone was quarried and brought down the canyon. It was dusty and dirty work, and made us sweat—it was of this earth—yet it was the necessary preparation for the mighty spiritual ordinances that are carried on daily in this magnificent temple. The endowment itself is symbolic; it is a series of symbols of vast realities, too vast for full understanding. Those who go through the temple and come out feeling that the service is unbeautiful have been so occupied with the outward form as to fail to understand the inner meaning. It is the meaning of things that counts in life.[1]

This brings me to a few words concerning symbolism. We live in a world of symbols. We know nothing, except by symbols. We make a few marks on a sheet of paper, and we say that they form a word which stands for love, or hate, or charity, or God, or eternity. The marks may not be very beautiful to the eye. No one finds fault with the symbols on the pages of a book because they are not as mighty in their own beauty as the things which they represent. We do not quarrel with the symbol "G-o-d" because it is not very beautiful, yet represents the majesty of God. We are glad to have symbols, if only the meaning of the symbols is brought home to us.

Following Elder Widtsoe's lead, the challenge is to bring the meaning of the symbols home to us.

Look beyond the Physical

To bring the meaning of the symbols of the temple home to us, we have to look beyond the physical. We've already touched on many lessons of symbolism, including the true meaning of words such as "Adam," "Michael," "token," and "endowment." To learn these deeper meanings, we went beyond what first met the eye or the ear. We went beyond what our society has taught us to see or hear, and we looked for what the Lord is trying to teach us to see and hear. Isaiah prophesied that the Savior Himself would not be recognized by many of His own because he did not appear spectacular to the natural man (Isaiah 53; Jacob 4:14). Because of this obsession with the physical or mechanical, many people looked right at their very Savior and somehow saw nothing of eternal significance. How incredibly tragic!

At the same time, the scriptures teach that all things bear witness of Christ, all things testify of Christ, and all things typify or represent Christ (2 Nephi 11:4; Alma 30:44; Moses 6:63). In other words, spiritual lessons are all around us if we will just open our spiritual eyes and ears. To avoid overlooking these great spiritual lessons that are veiled in symbols (especially in the temple), we again have to look beyond what first meets the eye.

Throughout the scriptures, the ordinances and covenants of the gospel, and the temple experience, there are greater meanings within the acts and words that are used to convey the message. Do not be discouraged or unimpressed by the form or wording of sacred actions and lessons that may not teach the casual observer. In other words, don't be a casual observer. Look deeper. Wade deeper into the waters. There are treasures, even hidden treasures, that await you if you truly want to find them. Again, nowhere is this process more prevalent or more powerful than in the temple.

A perfect example of looking beyond the physical and into the spiritual is the well-known painting of Moses ordaining Aaron outside of the Tabernacle. Moses is standing with his hands on Aaron's head, as Aaron is seated and wearing an elaborate breast-plate. The altar of sacrifice is to the right of the picture, in front of Aaron, and the laver for washing is to the left of the picture, behind Moses. Two men, most likely priests, stand behind Moses and the laver wearing white robes and colored aprons. To the rear of the picture, along the fabric borders of the tabernacle, many men stand wearing white robes and sashes that appear to be tied on the right side around their waists.

Notice that Aaron is holding a hat on his lap. The men behind Moses (again they are most likely intended by the artists to be priests) are wearing a similar hat.

When you look at Aaron's hat, what would you expect to see? Do you think of a turban worn by a middle eastern sheik or snake charmer? Does it look like something a pastry chef would wear? That's what our society would have us assume because we're just not used to seeing this sort of thing.

But if we look a little more carefully at the spiritual context of this hat, instead of the physical details that the world would have us notice and dwell on, we can see something more meaningful. In this case, the spiritual side is explained to us in the scriptures. Exodus 29:6 describes these priestly temple robes and instructs "thou shalt put the mitre upon his head, and put the holy crown upon the mitre." This hat worn by the priests was known as a mitre and was placed on the head to hold a crown in place. It also kept a metal crown from cutting into the royal head on which it was placed (Leviticus 8:9).

Now that we've looked beyond what first meets the eye, look again at the picture. Do you see the same strange hat? Or do you see the preparation and foundation for a crown? Do you see a king in waiting?

Think also of the famous scene in the *Ten Commandments* where Charlton Heston, acting as Moses, raises his arms and parts the Red Sea. Do you think of primitive but impressive Hollywood magic? Or do you think of chosen people being separated from bondage and captivity by parting and crossing water? Do you think of a symbol of baptism?

Think also of the famous temple scripture that prophesies about the return of Elijah. This scripture is so important that it's the only scripture found in all four of the standard works.

> For behold, the day cometh that shall burn as an oven, and all the proud, yea, and all that do wickedly shall burn as stubble; for they that come shall burn them, saith the Lord of Hosts, that it shall leave them neither root nor branch. . . .
>
> Behold, I will reveal unto you the Priesthood, by the hand of Elijah the prophet, before the coming of the great and dreadful day of the Lord. . . .
>
> And he shall plant in the hearts of the children the promises made to the fathers, and the hearts of the children shall turn to their fathers. If it were not so, the whole earth would be utterly wasted at his coming (Joseph Smith History 1:37–39).

When you read this scripture, do you think of a raging fire burning up trees? Look a little more closely, and you will see that the spiritual—the interpretation of the tree symbolism—is given within the scripture itself. When the scripture speaks of planting in the hearts of the children the promises made to the fathers and turning the hearts of the children to their fathers, do you make the connection between the root and branches mentioned earlier? Our roots are our fathers, and our branches are our children. Through the temple and the sealing power of Elijah in the temple, the blessings of eternal families are found. Here, like other lessons of the temple, those blessings are taught by the symbolism of a tree.

You just can't think of the temple in earthly terms. The Lord is trying to teach heavenly messages, and those just don't translate into earthly terms very well, especially when the world we're used to is more like Sodom than the City of Enoch. Look beyond what first meets the eye and what society has taught you to look for. Look instead for what the Lord is trying to teach you and rest assured that the lesson awaiting you is beautiful, wonderful, and profound.

MOUNTAINS

In identifying and putting together the pieces of the puzzle, it is helpful to understand that the scriptures give many temple experiences that aren't specifically labeled that way. Recognizing these as temple experiences not only teaches us more about the temple, but it also helps us understand what kind of experiences we should strive and long for in the temple.

As outlined in Chapter 3, most of these experiences happen on mountains. Mountains are literally the closest places to heaven on Earth. They are literally where heaven meets Earth. Altars convey the same symbolism on a smaller scale. Mountains are used as symbolic temples throughout the scriptures. For example, Moses saw the Lord through a burning bush on a mountain (Exodus 3).

In that experience, the Lord specifically told him to take off his shoes to show reverence because he was standing on holy ground (Exodus 3:5). If the Lord is speaking with His prophet and calling the place holy, we can be confident this is a temple experience. This is the kind of experience that happens in temples.

Later in Exodus, Moses received more specific instructions from the Lord in the form of the Ten Commandments (Exodus 20). This also happened on a mountain and was a temple experience.

Still later in Exodus, dozens of others were blessed to climb the mountain with Moses and see the Lord (Exodus 34). This temple experience shows us that we don't have to be a prophet in order to have the blessing of seeing the Lord.

In the Book of Mormon, the Brother of Jared saw the Lord, and the Lord pronounced him "redeemed from the fall" and brought into the presence of God (Ether 3:13). This great experience happened on a mountain and was also a temple experience. In this experience, the Lord pronounced the greatest of blessings on the Brother of Jared and confirmed that he had put the Atonement into full practice in his mortal life.

In the Pearl of Great Price, Moses was swept away to a mountain and was shown the Lord's infinite creations (see Moses 1). This too was a temple experience. In this experience, the Lord revealed His true nature and His works to Moses.

Not all temple experiences in the scriptures are so dramatic, however. In the Book of Mormon, the Lord commanded Nephi, "get thee into the mountain" (1 Nephi 17:7). When Nephi went to the mountain, the Lord commanded him to build a ship and showed him how to build it. This was not as momentous as the other temple experiences we've just discussed, and that is precisely the point. This example shows us that we can go to the Lord in the temple for help in our everyday lives. It also shows us that we don't have to see the face of the Lord to have a poignant temple experience. If we have a problem, even if it's about our worldly cares, the Lord is there for us in His mountain.

The scriptures are full of such experiences. Even when the

word *temple* is not mentioned, each of these temple experiences has a unique lesson for us that teaches the true purpose of temples and the blessings that are available to us in the temple. Generally speaking, when the Lord speaks directly with someone, or when man is fortunate enough to see the Lord's true nature and works, it is a temple experience. If the veil is being lifted or man is being redeemed from the Fall, then consider it a temple experience. Thinking symbolically, if heaven meets Earth in the scriptural experience, consider it a temple experience.

When you find such experiences in the scriptures, there is a lesson for you to seek the same kind of blessings and experiences in the temple today.

The Plan of Salvation in Symbols

There is a wonderful psalm in the Old Testament that displays the entire plan of salvation using symbols. We already discussed how the temple displays the plan of salvation using symbols, so there should be no surprise that this hymn of thanksgiving is centered on the temple. You might have read psalms like this in the scriptures without noticing the symbolism or the message in them. Now that we have discussed the principle of symbolism and have learned to look beyond what first meets the eye in search of the deeper meaning, this psalm is a great opportunity to apply these lessons.

In the Old Testament, Nehemiah was sent by Artaxerxes, a leader who was very good to the Jews, to rebuild the walls and gates of Jerusalem around 444 B.C. This was about ninety-two years after King Cyrus's first decree providing for the Jews to return to their native Jerusalem and begin reconstruction of the temple. When the task was completed, the Levites stood up and offered a wonderful psalm that marches us through the whole plan of salvation in symbols.

The Creation and Pre-mortal Existence—The psalm begins in verse five of chapter nine of Nehemiah.

Stand up and bless the Lord your God for ever and ever: and blessed be thy glorious name, which is exalted above all blessing and praise.

Thou, even thou, art Lord alone; thou hast made heaven, the heaven of heavens, with all their host, the earth, and all things that are therein, and the seas, and thou preservest them all; and the host of heaven worshippeth thee.

Thou art the Lord the God, who didst choose Abram, and broughtest him forth out of Ur of the Chaldees, and gavest him the name of Abraham.

And foundest his heart faithful before thee, and madest a covenant with him to give the land of the Canaanites, the Hittites, the Amorites, and the Perizzites, and the Jebusites, and the Girgashites, to give it, I say, to his seed, and hast performed thy words; for thou art righteous (Nehemiah 9:5–8).

This passage represents the Creation and the pre-mortal world (*See* D&C 93:29). Verse eight mentions the part of the Abrahamic covenant wherein the Lord promised a land for Abraham's seed to live in. This may seem like an odd place to speak of the Abrahamic covenant, but there are two spiritual lessons here. First, this scripture illustrates the eternal nature of covenants. We made covenants before we came to this Earth. Second, we came to Earth *because* of covenants we made earlier. Keeping our first estate provided us with an earthly home, just as Abraham's seed was promised a home because of the covenant.

Baptism—Continuing in verse nine, the psalm moves on to the next major step in the plan of salvation.

And didst see the affliction of our fathers in Egypt, and heardest their cry by the Red Sea;

And shewedst signs and wonders upon Pharaoh, and on all his servants, and on all the people of his land: for thou knewest that they dealt proudly against them. So didst thou get thee a name, as it is this day.

And thou didst divide the sea before them, so that they went through the midst of the sea on the dry land; and their persecutors thou threwest into the deeps, as a stone in the mighty waters (Nehemiah 9:9–11).

After the Creation and our birth, the next step in the plan of salvation is spiritual rebirth. In this passage, Egypt represents the world or the forbidden (Abraham 1:23). It is symbolically the place where the Lord was crucified (Revelation 11:8). We symbolically escape Egypt and Pharaoh and put off the natural man by exercising faith in the Lord Jesus Christ, repenting, and entering into the covenant of baptism. This is the first step toward becoming like God again. In doing so, we take upon ourselves the name of Christ (Mosiah 5:8). We divide the waters of baptism and leave the persecutors behind us.

The Strait and Narrow—After baptism we bear the name of Christ and are members of His church. After we have received this ordinance, we are to press forward, keeping the commandments and treasuring the word of God (2 Nephi 31:17–20). This is also the next principle in the psalm.

> Moreover thou leddest them in the day by a cloudy pillar; and in the night by a pillar of fire, to give them light in the way wherein they should go (Nehemiah 9:12).

The cloud by day and pillar by night represent the gift of the Holy Ghost. This gift is given immediately after baptism and gives us guidance in our everyday lives for as long as we're worthy of it.

The Temple—A new convert to the Church is eligible to enter the temple one year after baptism. If we are charting the essential ordinances of the Gospel, the temple would follow baptism. Not coincidentally, the temple comes next in the psalm.[2]

> Thou camest down also upon mount Sinai, and spakest with them from heaven, and gavest them right judgments, and true laws, good statutes and commandments;
> And madest known unto them thy holy sabbath, and commandedst them precepts, statutes, and laws, by the hand of Moses thy servant:
> And gavest them bread from heaven for their hunger, and broughtest forth water for them out of the rock for their thirst, and promisedst them that they should go in to possess the land which thou hadst sworn to give them (Nehemiah 9:13–15).

We recognize Mount Sinai as a temple. In fact, Mount Sinai was actually the site of many of the temple experiences we looked at earlier in this chapter. There are three specific temple lessons taught by this reference to Mount Sinai.

The first lesson, in verses 13 and 14, is that the temple is a place where higher laws are given. Those laws come to us through covenants. In the chapter on worthiness to enter the temple, we specifically looked at the Sabbath day as a preparatory commandment relating to the temple. We dedicate one day a week to the Lord so that we can prepare to dedicate seven days a week to Him. Here we see the same commandment and principle brought up again.

The second lesson, from verse 15, is the sacrament. It teaches the principle of always remembering Christ, who is the bread of life and the living water. Remember in the ancient temple that the emblems of the sacrament were found inside the holy place. Here we see the same emblems again as a reminder of our covenants and the Lord Jesus Christ.

The third lesson, also in verse 15, is the hope and goal of entering into the promised land. The temple exists to get us to the promised land and to make Adam become Michael again through the Atonement of the Son of God. We could also refer to the promised land as the tree of life, the Holy of Holies or the celestial kingdom. Returning there is the goal and promise of the psalm, the temple, and the plan of salvation.

Repentance and Enduring to the End—Notice that the psalm does not immediately take us to the promised land or the tree of life after it teaches the ordinances of the temple. In life, we are not immediately taken up to heaven after we receive our endowment. Sinai represents *making* certain covenants, and the next step in the psalm represents *keeping* those covenants throughout the period of trial that is mortality. This is a lifelong process that involves constant faith and repentance.

> But they and our fathers dealt proudly, and hardened their necks, and hearkened not to thy commandments,
> And refused to obey, neither were mindful of thy wonders that

thou didst among them; but hardened their necks, and in their rebel-
lion appointed a captain to return to their bondage: but thou art a
God ready to pardon, gracious and merciful, slow to anger, and of
great kindness, and forsookest them not.

Yea, when they had made them a molten calf, and said, This is
thy God that brought thee up out of Egypt, and had wrought great
provocations;

Yet thou in thy manifold mercies forsookest them not in the
wilderness: the pillar of the cloud departed not from them by day, to
lead them in the way; neither the pillar of fire by night, to shew them
light, and the way wherein they should go.

Thou gavest also thy good spirit to instruct them, and with-
heldest not thy manna from their mouth, and gavest them water for
their thirst.

Yea, forty years didst thou sustain them in the wilderness, *so
that* they lacked nothing; their clothes waxed not old, and their feet
swelled not. (Nehemiah 9:16–21).

Repentance is a lifelong principle, and the purification that
comes from it is a lifelong process. We cannot get back to the tree
of life without spending our lives in pursuit of it, and this means
we all need the blessing of repentance. We need it just as much
after we enter the temple as we did before we entered the temple.
As President Dieter Uchtdorf put it, "Remember, the heavens will
not be filled with those who never made mistakes but with those
who recognized that they were off course and who corrected their
ways to get back in the light of gospel truth."[3]

When we are off course and our necks are hardened (think
of the symbolism here—a stiff neck does not bow down or show
submissiveness), our Father in Heaven is still anxious to forgive us. Even when we get caught up in worshiping false gods
(worldliness), our Father is still anxious to bless us and provide
us with manna from heaven and water from the rock. In other
words, when we have strayed from our covenants, we can still
find redemption in the Atonement through the sacrament and
the renewal of our covenants.

The reference in verse 21 to forty years in the wilderness is
symbolic of the ultimate time of trial or proving. The flood of

Noah came with forty days and nights of rain. Christ fasted for forty days and nights before beginning His ministry. And, as referenced here, the children of Israel wandered in the wilderness forty years before Joshua took them into the promised land. The reference to clothes not wearing out and feet not swelling during this forty-year period is a reference to the Lord sustaining us through our trials, if we will only look to Him.[4] However long our "forty years in the wilderness" actually ends up lasting, if we endure to the end, keeping our covenants, then the blessings of the temple and the Atonement will allow us to enter the promised land with Jesus. The Holy Spirit of Promise will ratify our ordinances and seal the eternal reward that we have spent our lives diligently seeking.

Entering the Promised Land and Receiving the Blessings of the Abrahamic Covenant

The final step in the psalm depicts the blessings of entering the promised land.

> Moreover thou gavest them kingdoms and nations, and didst divide them into corners: so they possessed the land of Sihon, and the land of the king of Heshbon, and the land of Og king of Bashan.
>
> Their children also multipliedst thou as the stars of heaven, and broughtest them into the land, concerning which thou hadst promised to their fathers, that they should go in to possess it.
>
> So the children went in and possessed the land, and thou subduedst before them the inhabitants of the land, the Canaanites, and gavest them into their hands, with their kings, and the people of the land, that they might do with them as they would (Nehemiah 9:22–24).

This part of the psalm deals not just with entering the promised land, but also with the blessings of eternal posterity. These blessings go hand in hand. As part of the psalm, to enter the promised land is to receive the blessings of eternal posterity (See also Genesis 15:5; 17:8; Abraham 2:9; D&C 132:30). These are the blessings of the Abrahamic covenant and the blessings of exaltation. The plan of salvation is capped and crowned with the greatest of all gifts of God (D&C 14:7), as the children of the covenant enter into the promised land.[5] These blessings are only available through the temple. At the end of the psalm, the priests remind us what we have to do to receive these blessings. "And because of all this we make a sure covenant, and write it; and our princes, Levites, and priests, seal unto it" (Nehemiah 9:38). With that, I reiterate: It is not enough just to make covenants; we have to keep those covenants. The covenants and accompanying ordinances of the temple are the only way to put the Atonement into full practice in our lives and receive the greatest blessings of eternity.

Just as each part of this psalm teaches a part of the plan of salvation through symbolism, the temple also teaches the Plan, step by step, by using symbolism. Not all of the symbols in the temple are of the same type that we read here in this psalm, but the point is to identify the symbols and look more deeply to find the lessons that the Lord is teaching through those symbols. As you attend the temple, ponder the experiences you have there, and search the scriptures, the meaning of these symbols and their lessons about the Savior will be brought home to you. (See 3 Nephi 17:3.)

ANOTHER INVITATION:
WADE DEEPER AND KEEP GOING

The forty-seventh chapter of Ezekiel gives us a remarkably insightful lesson on the symbolism of the temple and what it takes to learn from that symbolism. In that chapter, Ezekiel is shown a vision of the temple that will one day be built in Jerusalem on Mount Zion. In this vision, Ezekiel sees a spring of pure water flowing from the foundation of the temple. The waters formed a river that ran into the Dead Sea and healed it, symbolically bringing life to the spiritually dead and everything in its wake.

In the vision, Ezekiel is instructed to walk into the river and test its depth. At first, the river only went to Ezekiel's ankles.

As Michael Wilcox puts it, an ankle-deep river is nothing to get excited about.[6] So, Ezekiel is told to wade a little farther down the river. This time, the waters went to Ezekiel's knees. As he went farther, the waters reached his loins. As he went a little farther still, the waters became "a river that I could not pass over: for the waters were risen, waters to swim in, a river that could not be passed over" (Ezekiel 47:3–5).

The message of Ezekiel's vision is to keep walking. If the temple at first seems as unimpressive as an ankle-deep river, just keep going. The farther we walk in the temple, the more life, healing, and understanding we will find from the rivers that flow from the temple.

SUMMARY

- The Lord uses symbolism to teach us great lessons because it has the unique ability to keep sacred things from those who are unprepared to receive them and reward those who are prepared to receive them.
- The temple is replete with symbolism. The challenge is for us to "bring home" the meaning of the symbols in the temple.
- To bring home the meaning of those symbols, we need to look beyond what first meets our eyes. We have been trained by our society to look at things a certain way, and we need to retrain ourselves to look at things the way the Lord looks at them. An understanding of this symbolism comes not just from retraining our minds but from the Holy Ghost.
- The scriptures contain many temple experiences that do not specifically happen in temples. Recognizing those experiences and their symbolism teaches us about the nature and purpose of the temple and helps us understand what kinds of experiences we should seek from the temple.

- If the temple seems as unimpressive to you as the ankle-deep river in Ezekiel's vision, just keep walking. The waters will get deeper and deeper and bring more and more healing and life to you.

Notes

1. John A. Widtsoe, "Temple Worship," *The Utah Geneaological and Historical Magazine*

2. In terms of ordinances, the next step for men would actually be ordination to the Priesthood. The psalm still fits because Melchizedek Priesthood ordination can properly be considered a prerequisite to, and a part of, the temple experience today.

3. Dieter F. Uchtdorf, "A Matter of a Few Degrees," *Ensign*, May, 2008.

4. By no coincidence, this is also the kind of blessing we can expect from keeping the law of tithing.

5. This is not the end of the psalm, but it is the pinnacle. The next several verses point out the problems encountered by the Israelites after they finally entered the promised land. Those verses recount how the Israelites lost their favored status by not honoring their covenants. In this sense, the rest of the psalm is a reminder of repentance and the need for a restoration.

6. S. Michael Wilcox, *House of Glory*, 40–43.

CHAPTER 10

THE ABRAHAMIC COVENANT AND THE TEMPLE

We have spent a great deal of time learning about Adam and his significance in the teachings of the temple. By now, we have learned well that we must consider ourselves as Adam and Eve as we make the journey back to the tree of life. But there is one other great and ancient prophet whose example is also critical to our understanding of the temple. He is Abraham.[1]

We are told by the Savior Himself that we should "do the works of Abraham" (John 8:39; D&C 132:32). In the previous chapter, we saw multiple references to Abraham and the Abrahamic covenant in the temple psalm. We saw that this covenant was used to describe the blessings of exaltation or of reaching the promised land. As this covenant is revealed in the temple, Abraham's covenant is found in many pieces of the puzzle, even if his specific name is not mentioned.

SEEKING AND FINDING THE LORD

Our first lesson on Abraham's role in the blessings of the temple begins in the Pearl of Great Price with chapter one of Abraham. Abraham explains:

> And, finding there was greater happiness and peace and rest for

me, I sought for the blessings of the fathers, and the right whereunto
I should be ordained to administer the same; having been myself
a follower of righteousness, desiring also to be one who possessed
great knowledge, and to be a greater follower of righteousness, and
to possess a greater knowledge, and to be a father of many nations,
a prince of peace, and desiring to receive instructions, and to keep
the commandments of God, I became a rightful heir, a High Priest,
holding the right belonging to the fathers. . . .

I sought for mine appointment unto the Priesthood according to
the appointment of God unto the fathers concerning the seed (Abraham 1:2, 4).

In chapter one, Abraham is seeking the Lord and these blessings of the Priesthood. In chapter two, he finds them.

My name is Jehovah, and I know the end from the beginning;
therefore my hand shall be over thee.

And I will make of thee a great nation, and I will bless thee
above measure, and make thy name great among all nations, and
thou shalt be a blessing unto thy seed after thee, that in their hands
they shall bear this ministry and Priesthood unto all nations;

And I will bless them through thy name; for as many as receive
this Gospel shall be called after thy name, and shall be accounted
thy seed, and shall rise up and bless thee, as their father;

And I will bless them that bless thee, and curse them that curse
thee; and in thee (that is, in thy Priesthood) and in thy seed (that is,
thy Priesthood), for I give unto thee a promise that this right shall
continue in thee, and in thy seed after thee (that is to say, the literal
seed, or the seed of the body) shall all the families of the earth be
blessed, even with the blessings of the Gospel, which are the blessings of salvation, even of life eternal.

Now, after the Lord had withdrawn from speaking to me, and
withdrawn his face from me, I said in my heart: Thy servant has
sought thee earnestly; now I have found thee (Abr. 2:8–12).[2]

Abraham spent the rest of his life fulfilling his part of the
covenant by walking before God and becoming perfect (Genesis
17:1).

Genesis 22 brings the account of the Abrahamic covenant full
circle. Years before, when Abraham was given pieces of the covenant, he was promised great posterity. At that time, he and Sarah

had no posterity, even though they had longed for children for decades. Years later, Abraham and Sarah received the beginning of their promised blessings with the birth of Isaac. They now had posterity, the very blessing they had sought and were promised earlier. Several years after this blessing of posterity had materialized, the Lord commanded the ultimate sacrifice of Abraham. He was to sacrifice the very blessing he and Sarah had longed for, for so many years. Asking Abraham to sacrifice Isaac was asking Abraham to sacrifice everything.

As it turned out, being willing to sacrifice the blessing they had sought and had at last received, only multiplied the blessing. After Abraham proved his willingness to sacrifice all things and obey the Lord at all costs, the promised blessing of eternal posterity was emphatically reiterated to Abraham but was even more glorious than before.

> And the angel of the LORD called unto Abraham out of heaven the second time,
> And said, By myself have I sworn, saith the LORD, for because thou hast done this thing, and hast not withheld thy son, thine only son:
> That in blessing I will bless thee, and in multiplying I will multiply thy seed as the stars of the heaven, and as the sand which is upon the sea shore; and thy seed shall possess the gate of his enemies;
> And in thy seed shall all the nations of the earth be blessed; because thou hast obeyed my voice (Genesis 22:15–18).

This illustrates how the principle of sacrifice works: You give up something so dear, and it comes back multiplied. The sacrifice of all things somehow multiplies the reward even further. Abraham had long been a righteous man, but when he proved himself willing to sacrifice all things, his promised blessing was emphatically multiplied in no uncertain terms.

How does this relate to the temple? This sacrifice is the most compelling illustration of the Atonement in all of scripture, and, not coincidentally, it took place where a temple would later be built (2 Chronicles 3:1). Like Abraham, God the Father gave His Only Begotten Son as a sacrifice for all the followers of Abraham and all the children of Adam. One precious, irreplaceable Son was offered as a sacrifice, and countless other sons and daughters were given life, even eternal life. However, unlike Abraham, it was not enough for the Father just to be willing to make the sacrifice. There was no ram in the thicket who could atone for the sins of the world. The Lamb of God was the only worthy sacrifice.

The connection between Abraham and the temple does not end at Mount Moriah. While Mount Moriah presents the most poignant illustration of the Atonement in all of scripture, it is much more than just an illustration. It is a covenant that we are all invited to share in. This is where Abraham's story, like Adam's, becomes our story. Through the temple, the blessings of the Abrahamic covenant are not restricted to just Abraham. As Abraham sought these blessings, so should we. Specifically, the blessings of the Priesthood sought and found by Abraham can be ours through the temple.[3] Moreover, the blessings of posterity as numerous as the sands of the seashore and the stars in the heavens can also be ours *only* through the temple.

Whether we realize it or not, these are the same blessings that are promised to us in the temple. Bruce R. McConkie tells us, "When he is married in the temple for time and all eternity, each worthy member of the Church enters personally into the same covenant the Lord made with Abraham. This is the occasion when the promises of eternal increase are made, and it is then specified that those who keep the covenants made there shall be inheritors of all the blessings of Abraham, Isaac, and Jacob."[4]

To this, the Lord adds:

> This promise is yours also, because ye are of Abraham, and the promise was made unto Abraham; and by this law is the continuation of the works of my Father, wherein he glorifieth himself.
>
> Go ye, therefore, and do the works of Abraham; enter ye into my law and ye shall be saved.
>
> But if ye enter not into my law ye cannot receive the promise of my Father, which he made unto Abraham (D&C 132:31–33).

Those who receive these blessings of the Abrahamic covenant are also described in section 76 of the Doctrine and Covenants as priests and kings—the female equivalent blessings are implied in this scripture even though it uses masculine nouns. This blessing and these titles are also part of the Abrahamic covenant.

> These are they who are priests and kings, who have received of his fullness, and of his glory;
> And are priests of the Most High, after the order of Melchizedek, which was after the order of Enoch, which was after the order of the Only Begotten Son.
> Wherefore, as it is written, they are gods, even the sons of God (D&C 76:56–58).

If you go to the temple—especially if you are being sealed to your precious spouse or family—without recognizing the role and blessings of the Abrahamic covenant, you have missed the point. The greatest eternal blessings promised to Abraham can belong to each of us through the temple. These blessings are the crowning achievement of mortality, and are the purpose of the temple experience. Abraham is not just a prophet; he is the example of the blessings of exaltation to everyone who enters the temple.

These blessings are not just enjoying the presence of God; they are being like God. With these blessings, the Fall is overcome. These blessings are the tree of life, the top of the mountain, the pinnacle of the temple experience and the fulfillment of the plan of salvation. Adam, through the Savior, has now become Michael. "For I am the Lord thy God, and will be with thee even unto the end of the world, and through all eternity; for verily I seal upon you your exaltation, and prepare a throne for you in the kingdom of my Father, with Abraham your father" (D&C 132:49).

SUMMARY

- Like Adam, Abraham is another example to follow in order to identify and put together the pieces of the puzzle and understand the blessings of the temple.
- These blessings are part of the Abrahamic covenant and are

only available through the temple. For us, these blessings are specifically the promise of eternal Priesthood and seed as numerous as the sands on the seashore and the stars in the heavens.

- These blessings also include being a priest and a king.
- To receive the fullness of the blessings of the temple, including the ordinance and blessings of celestial marriage, is to receive the blessings of the Abrahamic covenant. These blessings represent not just being with God but being like God. These blessings represent Adam becoming Michael, mankind becoming like God and partaking of the tree of life.

Notes

1. Just as the name "Adam" is meant to represent mankind in general, both masculine and feminine, we are really referring to both Abraham and Sarah when we speak of Abraham. The covenants and blessings that make Abraham so important to our understanding the temple all involve Sarah. There would be no Abrahamic covenant without Sarah. So when we refer to Abraham, Sarah's role is understood as a given.

2. Facsimile Two in the Book of Abraham also depicts Abraham receiving these blessings. Abraham is pictured as a king sitting upon the throne of Pharaoh, likely the most powerful man on Earth. Abraham is wielding a scepter that represents the Priesthood. In this depiction, Abraham is both a king and a priest.

3. Ezra Taft Benson, "What I Hope You Will Teach Your Children about the Temple," *Ensign*, Aug. 1985.

4. Bruce R. McConkie, *New Witness for the Articles of Faith*, 508.

Chapter 11

Assembling the Pieces of the Puzzle

In the individual chapters of this book, we have discussed a great many pieces of the puzzle. These pieces do indeed fit together, and they do indeed form a masterpiece rendition of heaven. However, to this point, we have grouped the pieces mostly by subject and not in chronological order. We've looked at important words, Adam and Eve, worthiness, blessings, covenants and ordinances, symbolism, and the Abrahamic covenant.

Now, if we arrange some of these pieces in a chronological or progressive order, much of the final product is revealed. This order begins with our preparation to enter the temple and follows through to the ancient temple, as it is revealed in the Old Testament and as explained in Elder Talmage's description of the endowment.

We start with our preparation to enter the temple. We learned of the importance of worthiness and some of the specific commandments we must be living in order to enter the temple. This is the foundation. It opens the doors of the temple.

We learned that before Aaron and the priests entered the tabernacle, they were washed and anointed (Exodus 29, 30). This washing represents cleansing, and the anointing represents being chosen. This is a birth of water and of the Spirit, much like baptism and confirmation and the sacrament. Baptism brings us into the Lord's church, and washing and anointing brings us into the

Lord's house. Think of this also as a kind of dedicatory prayer for your own temple.

Within the temple, the plan of salvation is presented from the perspective of Adam and Eve, starting with the Creation and then the Fall. Adam and Eve are our role models, and our eternal progression follows their pattern as we are taught in the temple.

In the Creation and pre-mortal existence, Adam was known as *Michael*, meaning "who is like God." This name represents our origin as children of God. When he was born and placed on the Earth, he was given the name *Adam*, which means "mankind." This name represents our present state. We also know that *Michael* is the post-mortal name of Adam. This name represents our eternal potential to return to God and be like Him. These name changes represent Adam's position and progress in the plan of salvation.

In the Fall, we saw the two trees: the tree of life representing the presence of God, and the tree of knowledge of good and evil representing mortality (2 Nephi 2:23). After Adam and Eve ate from the tree of knowledge of good and evil, they began mortality. The tree of life was then off-limits to them until they could be found worthy to return and eat from it. In order to protect Adam and Eve, the Lord placed cherubim and a flaming sword to guard the way of the tree of life until they could prove their worthiness to eat of the tree (Alma 42:4–5).

We learned that these cherubim guarding the path to the tree of life are our friends, not our enemies. We want to be worthy and able to pass them and eat again from the tree of life, but, as President Young summarized, we need certain signs and tokens in order to pass by them. These signs and tokens represent covenants made and kept. Specifically, a token is our proof of the covenants we have made.

Before Adam and Eve were cast out of the Garden of Eden, we read that the Lord made coats of skins for them (Genesis 3:21). He clothed them, and "to clothe" is one of the meanings of the word "endowment." This act of clothing was likely a great lesson to Adam and Eve about the principle of sacrifice, which points to the Atonement of Jesus Christ. The temple exists so that we may put the Atonement into full practice in our lives. The garments given to them by the Lord serves as a reminder of the Atonement and all that Adam and Eve needed to do to return to the tree of life.

Adam and Eve were then cast out into their period of mortality on the earth. To return to the tree of life, or to climb the ladder leading back to heaven, Adam and Eve needed to receive certain ordinances and make and keep certain covenants. Ordinances are outward acts that often teach symbolic lessons about the covenants that they accompany.

Some of these ordinances are given through the Aaronic Priesthood. Like the Mosaic law, the function of the Aaronic Priesthood is to prepare or to bring people to Christ. For example, baptism is an ordinance of the Aaronic Priesthood in which we covenant to take upon ourselves a new name, which is the name of Jesus Christ. Adam's journey toward becoming like God began when he received these ordinances and put off the natural man (Mosiah 3:19).

Once we are delivered to Christ's church through the ordinances of the Aaronic Priesthood, we are prepared to receive the higher ordinances and covenants of the Melchizedek Priesthood. This Priesthood and its ordinances and covenants have the power to take us back to the Father, or back to the tree of life. Each of these saving ordinances is a lesson about the Savior and embodies covenants that we must keep.

Making and keeping these covenants takes us up Jacob's ladder toward heaven (Genesis 28:12–22). Each of the covenants we make and keep takes us gradually from the terrestrial kingdom and eventually into the celestial kingdom. No one climbs Jacob's ladder alone. Divine messengers are ascending and descending on the ladder (Genesis 28:12). They are constantly offering help to us as we climb the ladder, whether we realize it or not.

As we saw in the ancient temple, the principles of sacrifice, obedience, and prayer are a common theme of this journey through mortality back to the Holy of Holies or tree of life. They are principles that mark each day in the life of a true follower or Christ. The sacrifices offered in the ancient temple were animals. The sacrifice required of us today is a broken heart and a contrite spirit (3 Nephi 9:19–20). If we truly offer this sacrifice, then we will be willing to offer any other sacrifice and obey any other commandment the Lord may give us, just like Abraham (Genesis 22).

We also saw in the ancient temple the emblems of the sacrament, which remind us of the importance of renewing our covenants each Sabbath day and living so that the Spirit of the Lord can be with us (Exodus 25:23–40). In these symbols, we find countless lessons on the Atonement.

We learned that just before the veil to the Holy of Holies, incense was burned, which represented the prayers of the righteous (Exodus 30:1–10). On the subject of prayers of the righteous, we also learned of an Old Testament practice of praying with hands reached toward heaven (1 Kings 8:38, 54; Psalms 141:2; Ezra 9:5; 1 Timothy 2:8; D&C 88:135) in the universal sign of surrender. In this case, the surrender is to the Lord. A person offering such a prayer leaves his heart, lips, hands, and mind in open view of the Father. As we learned in Psalms 24, these are the indicators of our worthiness to stand in the Lord's holy place. In this manner, the Father can openly judge a person's purity and worthiness to stand in His presence.

Cherubim guarded the entrance to the Holy of Holies in the ancient temple. They were woven into the veil or entry to the Holy of Holies (Exodus 26:31). The Holy of Holies also represents the tree of life or the celestial kingdom. Before we can actually enter the presence of the Father, we need to pass these cherubim, as explained in President Brigham Young's definition of the endowment. If we have made and thoroughly kept the covenants represented by the signs and tokens mentioned by President Young, then we have put the Atonement into full practice in our lives.

We saw when the Lord Jesus Christ finished paying the debt for our mortality that the veil in the temple was torn (Matthew 27:51). Symbolically and literally, the barrier between man and

God was broken by the Savior's Atonement. Through the Atonement, Adam can now return to, and be like, God. If we have put the Atonement into full practice by making and keeping the covenants of exaltation, we are prepared to pass the guardians and enter the Holy of Holies.

We also learned that the blessings of entering this most holy place are the blessings of the Abrahamic covenant (See Nehemiah 9: 22–24). To receive these blessings is not just to return to man's heavenly home, but to become like God. Receiving these blessings is the process and fulfillment of Adam becoming Michael.

My friends, do not be content with mortality and its rewards. They are *nothing* compared to the blessings of the temple. Live for the blessings of eternity and the blessings of becoming like God. Come to the House of the Lord. Make these covenants. Treasure these covenants each step of the way through mortality, and you will climb Jacob's ladder and will be lifted up by a power far beyond your own. Like Abraham, you will walk before God in mortality and become perfect, just as Christ taught us. You will return to your heavenly home and be like your Heavenly Father.

SELECTED BIBLIOGRAPHY

BOOKS

Alfred Edersheim, *The Temple—Its Ministry and Services as They Were at the Time of Christ* (Grand Rapids: Wm. B. Eerdmans Publishing Co, 1990).

Alonzo Gaskill, *The Lost Language of Symbolism* (Salt Lake City: Deseret Book, 2003).

Alonzo Gaskill, *The Savior and the Serpent* (Salt Lake City: Deseret Book, 2005).

Dean C. Jessee, ed. *The Personal Writings of Joseph Smith* (Salt Lake City: Deseret Book, 1984).

Bruce R. McConkie, *New Witness for the Articles of Faith* (Salt Lake City: Bookcraft, 1986).

Joseph Fielding McConkie, *Gospel Symbolism* (Salt Lake City: Deseret Book, 1985).

Joseph Fielding McConkie & Donald W. Parry, *A Guide to Scriptural Symbols* (Salt Lake City: Bookcraft, 1990).

Mark L. McConkie, ed., *Doctrines of the Restoration: Sermons and Writings of Bruce R. McConkie* (Salt Lake City: Bookcraft, 1989).

Jacob Neusner, *Neusner on Judaism Vol. 3, Religion and Theology*

(Burlington: Ashgate Publishing, 2006).

Hugh Nibley, *Mormonism and Early Christianity* (Salt Lake City: Deseret Book, 1987).

Oxford English Dictionary, 1989 ed.

Donald W. Parry, ed., *Temples of the Ancient World: Ritual and Symbolism* (Salt Lake City: F.A.R.M.S., 1994).

Evan Tye Peterson, ed., *The Ninth Temple—A Light in the Desert* (Orem: Granite Publishing, 2002).

Joseph Smith, *Lectures on Faith* (Salt Lake City: Bookcraft, 1959).

Joseph F. Smith, *Gospel Doctrine* (Salt Lake City: Bookcraft, 1939).

Joseph Fielding Smith, ed., *Teachings of the Prophet Joseph Smith* (Salt Lake City: Deseret Book, 1938).

Joseph Fielding Smith, *Doctrines of Salvation, Vol. 2* (Salt Lake City: Bookcraft, 1955).

James Strong, *Strong's Exhaustive Concordance of the Bible* (Iowa Falls: World Bible Publishers, 1989).

James E. Talmage, *The House of the Lord* (Salt Lake City: Deseret Book, 1974).

Elden J. Watson, ed., *Manuscript History of Brigham Young, 1846–1847* (Salt Lake City: Smith Secretarial Service, 1968).

Webster's New World Dictionary of the American Language, 1962 Ed.

John A. Widtsoe, ed. *Discourses of Brigham Young* (Salt Lake City: Deseret Book, 1926).

S. Michael Wilcox, *House of Glory* (Salt Lake City: Deseret Book, 1995).

Articles

Ezra Taft Benson, "What I Hope You Will Teach Your Children about the Temple." *Ensign,* Aug. 1985, 6.

C. Wilfred Griggs, "The Tree of Life in Ancient Cultures." *Ensign,* June, 1988, 27.

Gordon B. Hinckley, "This Thing Was Not Done in a Corner." *Ensign,* Nov. 1996, 48.

Howard W. Hunter, "Exceeding Great and Precious Promises." *Ensign,* July 1994, 21.

Russell M. Nelson, *Church News,* October 31, 1992.

Donald W. Parry, "Temple Worship and a Possible Reference to a Prayer Circle in Psalm 24." *BYU Studies 32/4* (1992), 57–62.

Marion G. Romney, "Temples–The Gates to Heaven," *Ensign,* Mar. 1971, 12.

Dieter F. Uchtdorf, "A Matter of a Few Degrees," *Ensign,* May 2008, 60.

John A. Widtsoe, "Temple Worship," *The Utah Geneaological and Historical Magazine* 12 (April 1921).

ABOUT THE AUTHOR

Mark Shields has been happily married to his wife, the former Cami Chamberlain, since 1992. They are the proud parents of five daughters: Heidi, Kayla, Claire, Anna, and Robyn. He is currently serving as bishop of his ward in Mesa, Arizona. He has served as an instructor for many temple preparation classes, missionary preparation classes, missionary training center classes, Primary and nursery classes, and Gospel Doctrine and Gospel Essentials classes. He has also served as a high councilor, a seminary teacher, and a temple worker.

0 26575 52873 2